First World War
and Army of Occupation
War Diary
France, Belgium and Germany

36 DIVISION
Divisional Troops
122 Field Company Royal Engineers
4 October 1915 - 28 February 1919

WO95/2497/2

The Naval & Military Press Ltd
www.nmarchive.com
Published in association with The National Archives

Published by

The Naval & Military Press Ltd

Unit 10 Ridgewood Industrial Park,

Uckfield, East Sussex,

TN22 5QE England

Tel: +44 (0) 1825 749494

www.naval-military-press.com

www.nmarchive.com

This diary has been reprinted in facsimile from the original. Any imperfections are inevitably reproduced and the quality may fall short of modern type and cartographic standards.

© **Crown Copyright**
Images reproduced by permission of The National Archives, London, England, 2015.

Contents

Document type	Place/Title	Date From	Date To
Heading	WO95/2497/2 122 Field Company Royal Engineers		
Heading	36th Division 122nd Field Coy R.E. Oct 1915-Feb 1919		
Heading	36th Division 122nd Loy F C R E Vol I Oct 15		
Heading	Confidential-War Diary of 122nd Field Company RE From 4/10/15 to 31/10/15 Volume 1		
War Diary	Bordon	04/10/1915	04/10/1915
War Diary	Havre	05/10/1915	06/10/1915
War Diary	Mirvaux	07/10/1915	11/10/1915
War Diary	Arqueves	12/10/1915	15/10/1915
War Diary	Toutencourt	16/10/1915	31/10/1915
Heading	36th Division 122nd F.C.R.E. Vol 2 121/7761 Nov 15		
Heading	Confidential War Diary of 122nd Field Coy R.E. from 1 November 1915 to 30 November 1915 (Volume 2)		
War Diary	Toutencourt	01/11/1915	07/11/1915
War Diary	Mailly-Maillet	08/11/1915	13/11/1915
War Diary	Englebelmer	08/11/1915	13/11/1915
War Diary	Mesnil	08/11/1915	13/11/1915
War Diary	Toutencourt	14/11/1915	30/11/1915
Heading	36th Div 122nd F.C.R.E. Vol 3 121/7931		
Heading	Confidential War Diary of 122 Field Co R.E. Volume 3		
War Diary	Toutencourt	01/12/1915	20/12/1915
War Diary	Beauval	21/12/1915	21/12/1915
War Diary	Pont-Remy	21/12/1915	27/12/1915
War Diary	Beauval	21/12/1915	31/12/1915
Heading	36 122nd F.C.R.E. Vol 4		
Heading	Confidential War Diary of 122nd Field Coy R.E. From 1st January 1916 to 31st January (Volume 4)		
War Diary	Beauval	01/01/1916	31/01/1916
War Diary	Terramesnil	31/01/1916	31/01/1916
Heading	Confidential War Diary of 122nd Field Company R.E. From 1/2/16 to 29/2/16 Volume 5		
War Diary	Beauval	01/02/1916	03/02/1916
War Diary	Englebelmer	04/02/1916	29/02/1916
Heading	War Diary of 122nd Field Coy RE from March 1st 1916 to March 31st 1916 Volume 6		
War Diary	Englebelmer H Mesnil	01/03/1916	06/03/1916
War Diary	Englebelmer	07/03/1916	07/03/1916
War Diary	Martinsart	07/03/1916	07/03/1916
War Diary	Englebelmer	08/03/1916	12/03/1916
War Diary	Englebelmer	13/03/1916	27/03/1916
War Diary	Forceville	28/03/1916	28/03/1916
War Diary	Aveluy	28/03/1916	28/03/1916
War Diary	Aveluy	29/03/1916	31/03/1916
Heading	War Diary of 122nd Field Coy RE from April 1st 1916 to April 30th 1916 Volume 7		
War Diary	Forceville	01/04/1916	01/04/1916
War Diary	Aveluy	01/04/1916	01/04/1916
War Diary	Mesnil	02/04/1916	03/04/1916
War Diary	Mesnil	03/04/1916	08/04/1916

War Diary	Martinsart	09/04/1916	09/04/1916
War Diary	Forceville	10/04/1916	30/04/1916
War Diary	Aveluy	10/04/1916	30/04/1916
War Diary	Martinsart	30/04/1916	30/04/1916
War Diary	Mesnil	30/04/1916	30/04/1916
Heading	War Diary of 122nd Field Company R.E. Period May 1st 1916 to May 31st 1916 Volume 8		
War Diary	Forceville	01/05/1916	01/05/1916
War Diary	Aveluy Wood	01/05/1916	01/05/1916
War Diary	Mesnil	01/05/1916	01/05/1916
War Diary	Martinsart Wood	01/05/1916	10/05/1916
War Diary	Forceville	11/05/1916	11/05/1916
War Diary	Aveluy Wood	11/05/1916	11/05/1916
War Diary	Mesnil	11/05/1916	11/05/1916
War Diary	Martinsart Wood	11/05/1916	31/05/1916
Heading	36th Divisional Engineers 122nd Field Company R.E. June 1916		
Heading	War Diary of 122nd Field Company R.E. Period June 1st 1916 to June 30th 1916 Volume 9		
War Diary	Martinsart	01/06/1916	22/06/1916
War Diary	Aveluy Wood	01/06/1916	22/06/1916
War Diary	Thiepval Wood	01/06/1916	22/06/1916
War Diary	Mound Keep	23/06/1916	30/06/1916
Heading	36th Divisional Engineers 122nd Field Company R.E. July 1916		
War Diary	War Diary of 122nd Field Coy R.E. From 1st July 1916 to 31st July 1916 Volume 10		
War Diary	Mound Keep (Q. 35 b. 5.1.)	01/07/1916	31/07/1916
Heading	War Diary of 122nd Field Coy R.E. From August 1st 1916 to August 31st 1916 Volume 11		
War Diary	Red Looge	01/08/1916	31/08/1916
War Diary	War Diary of 122 Field Company R.E. From 1st September to 30th September 1916 Volume 12		
War Diary	Red Looge	01/09/1916	30/09/1916
Heading	War Diary of 122nd Field Coy R.E-36th Division from October 1st 1916 to October 31st 1916 Volume 13		
War Diary	Red Looge	01/10/1916	03/10/1916
War Diary	Le Romarin	01/10/1916	03/10/1916
War Diary	Rea Looge	03/10/1916	03/10/1916
War Diary	Petit Pont	04/10/1916	31/10/1916
War Diary	War Diary of 122nd Field Company RE 36 Division from November 1st 1916 to November 30th 1916 Volume 14		
War Diary	Petit Pont	01/11/1916	01/11/1916
War Diary	Le Row Area	01/11/1916	01/11/1916
War Diary	Petit Pont	01/11/1916	30/11/1916
Heading	War Diary of 122nd Field Company RE 36th Division from December 1st 1916 to December 31st 1916 Volume 15		
War Diary	Petit Pont	01/12/1916	01/12/1916
War Diary	Le Romarin Petit Pont	01/12/1916	29/12/1916
War Diary	Petit Pont	30/12/1916	30/12/1916
War Diary	War Diary of 122nd Field Company R.E. 36th Division from January 1st 1917 to January 31st 1917 Volume 16		
War Diary	Petit Pont	01/01/1917	26/01/1917

War Diary	War Diary of 122nd Field Company 36th Division from February 1st 1917 to February 28th 1917 Volume 17		
War Diary	Dranoutre	01/02/1917	28/02/1917
Heading	War Diary 122nd Field Company R.E. 36th Division from March 1st 1917 to March 31st 1917 Volume 18		
War Diary	Neuve Eglise	01/03/1917	31/03/1917
War Diary	War Diary of 122nd Field Company R.E.36th Division from April 1st 1917 to April 30th 1917 Volume 19		
War Diary	Lindenhoek	01/04/1917	30/04/1917
Heading	War Diary of 122nd Field Coy R.E. 36th Div From 01/05/17 to 31/0517 Volume 20		
War Diary	Lindenhoek	01/05/1917	31/05/1917
Heading	War Diary of 122nd Field Company R.E. From June 1st 1917 to June to 30th 1917 Volume 21		
War Diary	Happy Valley Camp 28. S.W. 26. A. 7.1	01/06/1917	04/06/1917
War Diary	Happy Valley Camp	05/06/1917	08/06/1917
War Diary	Dranoutre	09/06/1917	10/06/1917
War Diary	N 55 D 21	13/06/1917	14/06/1917
War Diary	Happy Valley Camp	19/06/1917	30/06/1917
Heading	War Diary of 122nd Field Company R.E. From July 1st 1917 to July 31st 1917 Volume 22		
War Diary	Poperinge	01/07/1917	01/07/1917
War Diary	Winnezeele	02/07/1917	31/07/1917
Heading	War Diary of 122nd Field Coy. R.E. from 1st August 1917 to 31st August 1917 Volume 23		
War Diary	L. 16. A Central Sheet 27	01/08/1917	04/08/1917
War Diary	Ypres	04/08/1917	17/08/1917
War Diary	Winnezeele	18/08/1917	22/08/1917
War Diary	Ole Wood.	23/08/1917	23/08/1917
War Diary	Le Transloy	25/08/1917	29/08/1917
War Diary	Ruyaulcourt	30/08/1917	31/08/1917
Miscellaneous	O.C. 121 FA Co RE O.C. 122 FA Co RE	17/08/1917	17/08/1917
Heading	War Diary of 122nd Field Coy. R.E. 36 Division from 1st September 1917 to 30th Sept 1917 Volume 24		
War Diary	Ruyaulcourt	01/02/1917	28/02/1917
War Diary		29/02/1916	29/02/1916
War Diary		26/02/1916	26/02/1916
Heading	War Diary of 122nd Field Coy. R.E. 36 Division from 1st October 1917 to 31st October 1917 Volume 25		
War Diary	Ruyaulcourt.	01/10/1917	31/10/1917
Heading	War Diary of 122nd Field Coy. R.E. 36th Division From 1st Nov. 1917 to 30th Nov. 1917 Volume 26		
War Diary	Ruyaulcourt	01/11/1917	16/11/1917
War Diary	I 29 d 9.2	16/11/1917	20/11/1917
War Diary	Hermies J 29 b 5.7	20/11/1917	28/11/1917
Heading	Hermies	29/11/1917	29/11/1917
War Diary	J 30 a 6.4	30/11/1917	30/11/1917
Heading	War Diary of 122nd Field Company R.E. 36 Division From 1st December 1917 to 31st December 1917 Volume 27		
War Diary	Hermies	01/12/1917	04/12/1917
War Diary	Dessart Wood	05/12/1917	06/12/1917
War Diary	Havrincourt Wood Q 15. B	07/12/1917	10/12/1917
War Diary	Metz	11/12/1917	17/12/1917
War Diary	Etricourt	18/12/1917	18/12/1917
War Diary	Grincourt	19/12/1917	19/12/1917

War Diary	Pas	20/12/1917	28/12/1917
War Diary	Hailles	29/12/1917	31/12/1917
Heading	War Diary of 122nd Field Coy R.E. 36th Division From 1st January 1918 to 31st January 1918 Volume 28		
War Diary	Hailles	01/01/1918	07/01/1918
War Diary	Bayonvillers.	08/01/1918	10/01/1918
War Diary	Carrepuis	11/01/1918	12/01/1918
War Diary	Dury	13/01/1918	16/01/1918
War Diary	Bray St Christophe	17/01/1918	31/01/1918
Heading	War Diary of 122nd Field Coy Royal Engineers 36th Div. From 1/2/18 to 28/2/18 Volume 29		
War Diary	Bray St Christophe	01/02/1918	21/02/1918
War Diary	Grand Seraucourt G 9 C 1.4	22/02/1918	28/02/1918
War Diary	36th Divisional Engineers 122nd Field Company R.E. March 1918		
Heading	War Diary of 122nd Field Coy R.E. March 1918		
War Diary	G 9 C 14	01/03/1918	31/03/1918
Heading	36th Divisional Engineers 122nd Field Company R.E. April 1918		
Heading	War Diary of the 122nd Field Company Royal Engineers 36th Div From 1st April 1918 to 30th 1918 Vol 31		
War Diary	Dargnies	01/04/1918	04/04/1918
War Diary	Roex Poede Near Bergues	04/04/1918	04/04/1918
War Diary	Herzeele	05/04/1918	07/04/1918
War Diary	Ilminster Camp Near Wieltje	08/04/1918	15/04/1918
War Diary	Yser Canal Bank	16/04/1918	30/04/1918
Heading	War Diary of the 122nd Field Company Royal Engineers 36th Div. From May 1st to May 31st 1918		
War Diary		01/05/1918	31/05/1918
Heading	War Diary of 122nd Field Coy Royal Engineers 36 Div From 1st June to 30th june 1918 Vol 33		
War Diary	Hospital Farm Camp	01/06/1918	03/06/1918
War Diary	Ball Camp	04/06/1918	04/06/1918
War Diary	(L3 B 7.8)	05/06/1918	10/06/1918
War Diary	Ball Camp	11/06/1918	11/06/1918
War Diary	Price Camp	12/06/1918	13/06/1918
War Diary	Proven	14/06/1918	14/06/1918
War Diary	(F.7.b.5.2)	15/06/1918	22/06/1918
War Diary	Price Camp	23/06/1918	23/06/1918
War Diary	Proven (F.7.b.5.2)	24/06/1918	30/06/1918
Heading	War Diary of 122nd Field Coy Royal Engineers 36 Div From 1st July to 31st July 1918 Vol 34		
War Diary		01/07/1918	01/07/1918
War Diary	St Jan-De Bizen	02/07/1918	02/07/1918
War Diary	Eecke	03/07/1918	08/07/1918
War Diary	Mont-De-Cats.	08/07/1918	23/07/1918
War Diary	Le Lavriet	24/07/1918	31/07/1918
Heading	War Diary of 122nd Field Coy Royal Engineers 36 Div From 1st August to 31st August 1918 Vol 35		
War Diary	Eecke	01/08/1918	06/08/1918
War Diary	Mont Des Cats	07/08/1918	12/08/1918
War Diary	Mt Des Cast	13/08/1918	20/08/1918
War Diary	Mt Noir	21/08/1918	30/08/1918
Heading	War Diary of 122nd Field Coy Royal Engineers 36 Div From 1st September to 30th june 1918 Vol 35		

War Diary	Field	01/09/1918	30/09/1918
Heading	War Diary of 122nd Field Coy Royal Engineers 36 Div From 1st Oct to 30th Oct 1918 Vol 37		
War Diary Miscellaneous	Field	01/10/1918	31/10/1918
Heading	War Diary of 122nd Field Company R.E. 36th Division From 1st November to 30th November 1918 Vol 38		
War Diary	Lauwe S28/R24a 5.7	01/11/1918	03/11/1918
War Diary	Mouscron	04/11/1918	04/11/1918
War Diary	S 29/V 8 d 9/18	05/11/1916	05/11/1916
War Diary	Sheet 29	06/11/1918	09/11/1918
War Diary	Autryve S29/V8 d 9.8	10/11/1918	17/11/1918
War Diary	Mouscron S29/s23 a 5.6	18/11/1918	30/11/1918
Heading	War Diary of the 122nd Field Company R.E. 36th Division From 1st December 31st December 1918 Vol 39		
War Diary	Mouscron S29/S2 a 5.6	01/12/1918	31/12/1918
Heading	War Diary of the 122nd Field Company R.E. 36th Division From 1st January 31st January 1919 Vol 40		
War Diary	Mouscron	01/01/1919	31/01/1919
Heading	War Diary of the 122nd Field Company R.E. From 1st February to February 28 1919 Vol 41		
War Diary	Mouscron	01/02/1919	28/02/1919

WO/65/2497/2

122 Field Company Royal
Engineers

36TH DIVISION

122ND FIELD COY R.E.
OCT 1915 - FEB 1919

36TH DIVISION

121/7434

36th Burma

122nd Regt: FF&F.
Vol I
Oct 15

Army Form C. 2118.

(R)

WAR DIARY
or
~~INTELLIGENCE SUMMARY.~~
(Erase heading not required)

Instructions regarding War Diaries and Intelligence Summaries are contained in F. S. Regs., Part II and the Staff Manual respectively. Title pages will be prepared in manuscript.

Place	Date	Hour	Summary of Events and Information	Remarks and references to Appendices
			— Confidential — War Diary — of — 122nd Field Company R E from 4/10/15 to 31/10/15 — Volume 1 —	

Army Form C. 2118.

WAR DIARY
or
INTELLIGENCE SUMMARY.

(Erase heading not required.)

Instructions regarding War Diaries and Intelligence Summaries are contained in F. S. Regs., Part II. and the Staff Manual respectively. Title pages will be prepared in manuscript.

Place	Date	Hour	Summary of Events and Information	Remarks and references to Appendices
BORDON	4/7/15	—	Company entrained in 2 Echelons Arrived SOUTHAMPTON, detrained and embarked for HAVRE. 200 mounted branch with 2 officers embarking in S.S. EMPRESS QUEEN. H. officers, mounted branch & animals & transport in NORTH WESTERN MILLER	@ @
HAVRE	5/7/15	—	Arrived at HAVRE, disembarked and proceeded to No 5 REST CAMP	@
"	6/7/15	—	Entrained for LONGEAU	
MIRVAUX	7/7/15	—	Detrained at LONGEAU, and proceeded by march route through AMIENS to MIRVAUX	@
"	8/7/15 to 11/7/15	—	Billeted at MIRVAUX and proceeding with training of company. In the same area as 108th Brigade	@
ARQUÈVES	12/7/15	—	Proceeded by march route to ARQUÈVES where we joined Headquarters 26th Div. Eng: and the 121st and 130th Field Coys R.E.	@
"	13/7/15	—	At ARQUÈVES	
"	14/7/15	—	Sections marched over to TOUTENCOURT and worked on training for the defence of that village	@
"	15/7/15	—	ditto	@
TOUTENCOURT	16/7/15	—	Proceeded by march route to TOUTENCOURT and collected billets there	
"	17/7/15 to 23/7/15	—	Continuing with the defences of TOUTENCOURT and other works. These are part of the Brony line and those allotted to this company consist of defence localities IV, V and VI	@
"	24/7/15	—	2 Coys and of the 10th Labour Battalion marched over from HERISSART to assist the 122nd Company in these defensive works	@
"	25/7/15 to 31/7/15	—	Proceeding with these defences. 2 Coys from 10 Labour Battalion marching over daily.	@

122 md FCRF.
Vol. 2

1914/121

36th November

Nov 15.

Army Form C. 2118

WAR DIARY
or
INTELLIGENCE SUMMARY.
(Erase heading not required.)

CONFIDENTIAL
WAR DIARY
of
122nd Field Coy R.E.

from 1 November 1915 to 30 November 1915.

(Volume 2.)

Army Form C. 2118

WAR DIARY
or
INTELLIGENCE SUMMARY.
(Erase heading not required.)

Instructions regarding War Diaries and Intelligence Summaries are contained in F.S. Regs., Part II and the Staff Manual respectively. Title pages will be prepared in manuscript.

Place	Date	Hour	Summary of Events and Information	Remarks and references to Appendices
TOUTENCOURT	1/11/15 to 7/11/15		Proceeding with defence of TOUTENCOURT and neighbouring works, viz Army line defences localities IV V VI 122nd Field Coy R.E. assisted daily by B and C Companies of the 10th Labour Battalion.	
"			Arranged communication trenches from 3rd line of work IV to forward works of the French line for the defence of AMIENS	
MAILLY-MAILLET	8/11/15 to 13/11/15		Company proceeded by march route to MAILLY-MAILLET. Headquarters and Nos 2 and 3 Sections entered billets there and were attached to 9th Field Coy R.E. for instruction, working in first and second line trenches	
ENGLEBELMER	8/11/15 to 13/11/15		No.1 Section proceeded by march route to ENGLEBELMER and entered billets there, were attached to 1st West Lancs Field Coy R.E. for instruction, working in first and second line trenches. Billets occupied by No.1 Section in ENGLEBELMER were shelled by enemy. Three men slightly wounded by shell fragments.	
MESNIL	8/11/15 to 13/11/15		No.4 Section proceeded by march route to MESNIL and entered billets there, were attached to 1st West Lancs Field Coy R.E. for instruction, working in first and second line trenches	
TOUTENCOURT	14/11/15		Company proceeded by march route to TOUTENCOURT and entered billets there. Continuing with defence of localities IV V VI assisted daily by B and C Companies of the 10th Labour Battalion	
"	25/11/15 to 26/11/15		Took over works VII and VIII from 150th Field Coy R.E.	
"	27/11/15 to 30/11/15		Proceeding with defence of TOUTENCOURT and neighbouring works, localities IV V VI VII VIII assisted by B and C Companies of 10th Labour Battalion.	

Major R.E.
O.C. 182 By Field Coy R.E.

129 ⅏ F.C.R.E.
1943

19/4/43
12/1

36/4/43

Army Form C. 2118

WAR DIARY
or
INTELLIGENCE SUMMARY.

(Erase heading not required.)

Instructions regarding War Diaries and Intelligence Summaries are contained in F. S. Regs., Part II. and the Staff Manual respectively. Title pages will be prepared in manuscript.

Place	Date	Hour	Summary of Events and Information	Remarks and references to Appendices

Confidential

WAR DIARY.

of.

122 Field Co R.E

Volume 3.

Army Form C. 2118

WAR DIARY
or
INTELLIGENCE SUMMARY.
(Erase heading not required.)

Place	Date	Hour	Summary of Events and Information	Remarks and references to Appendices
TOUTENCOURT	1/12/15 – 20/12/15		Working on Army Line trenches defending village of TOUTENCOURT.	J.F.J.
	20/12/15		Handed over work to 10th Labour Battalion	J.F.J.
BEAUVAL	21/12/15		Proceeded by route march to BEAUVAL. Headquarters and Hay Coy reported to J.F.J. C.E. 13th Corps for work under him	J.F.J.
PONT-REMY	21/12/15 – 27/12/15		Hay Coy proceeded by route march to PONT REMY and reported to C.R.E. for work under him.	
BEAUVAL	21/12/15 – 31/12/15		rejoining Headquarters at BEAUVAL. Working in BEAUVAL. opening workshops. Cutting and collecting timber and other building material. Preparing BEAUVAL for troops.	

Morshi
Major RE
O.C. 122nd Field Coy RE

122nd FCLE.
Vol: 4

36

CONFIDENTIAL

WAR DIARY

of

122nd Field Coy R.E.

from 1st January 1916 to 31st January 1916.

(Volume IV)

Army Form C. 2118.

WAR DIARY
or
INTELLIGENCE SUMMARY.
(Erase heading not required.)

Instructions regarding War Diaries and Intelligence Summaries are contained in F. S. Regs., Part II. and the Staff Manual respectively. Title pages will be prepared in manuscript.

Place	Date	Hour	Summary of Events and Information	Remarks and references to Appendices
BEAUVAL	1/1/16		Working under C.E. 13th Corps on Hutting Scheme in BEAUVAL	
"	3/1/16			
"	3/1/16		"A" Coy 14th R.I.R. reported for work on Hutting Scheme	
"	15/1/16		"A" Coy 8th A. & S.H. started for work on Hutting Scheme	
"	26/1/16		"A" Coy 14th R.I.R. withdrawn from work on Hutting Scheme	
"	26/1/16		"C" Coy 11th R.I.R. reported for work on Hutting Scheme	
"	31/1/16		"A" Coy 8th A. & S.H. withdrawn from work on Hutting Scheme	
TERRAMESNIL	31/1/16		No. 2 Section proceeded from BEAUVAL to TERRAMESNIL by route march, in work on Hutting Scheme there	

Army Form C. 2118.

WAR DIARY
or
INTELLIGENCE SUMMARY.
(Erase heading not required.)

Place	Date	Hour	Summary of Events and Information	Remarks and references to Appendices
				122/728/ Vol 5

— CONFIDENTIAL —

War Diary
of
122ⁿᵈ Field Company R.E.

from 1-2-16 to 29-2-16

— Volume 5 —

Army Form C. 2118.

WAR DIARY
or
INTELLIGENCE SUMMARY.
(Erase heading not required.)

Instructions regarding War Diaries and Intelligence Summaries are contained in F.S. Regs., Part II. and the Staff Manual respectively. Title pages will be prepared in manuscript.

Place	Date	Hour	Summary of Events and Information	Remarks and references to Appendices
BEAUVAL	1/2 to 3/2	—	Working on 3rd Army Felting Scheme.	(1)
ENGLEBELMER	4/2	—	Headquarters and 3 sections moved to ENGLEBELMER.	(1a)
"	5/2 to 12/2	—	Working on front, second and Divisional line trenches in area occupied by 108rd Infantry Brigade — Revision and construction of trenches. Construction of new infantry dugouts.	(1a)
"	13/2 to 19/2	—	Continuation of this work.	(1b)
"	20/2 to 26/2	—	Continuation of this work.	(1c)
"	27/2 to 29/2	—	Continuation of this work.	(1d)

[signature]
Major R.E.
O.C. 122nd Field Coy R.E.
36th Division

122 F.C.R.E.
Vol 6

Army Form C. 2118.

WAR DIARY
or
INTELLIGENCE SUMMARY.
(Erase heading not required.)

XXXV

CONFIDENTIAL

WAR DIARY
OF
122ᵗʰ Field Coy. R.E.

From March 1ˢᵗ 1916 to March 31ˢᵗ 1916

Volume 6

Place	Date	Hour	Summary of Events and Information	Remarks and references to Appendices

Army Form C. 2118.

WAR DIARY
or
INTELLIGENCE SUMMARY.
(Erase heading not required.)

Instructions regarding War Diaries and Intelligence Summaries are contained in F.S. Regs., Part II and the Staff Manual respectively. Title pages will be prepared in manuscript.

Place	Date	Hour	Summary of Events and Information	Remarks and references to Appendices
ENGLEBELMER & MESNIL	1/7/16 to 5/7/16	—	Hq Qrs + 3 sections at ENGLEBELMER. 1 section at MESNIL. Working on front + support line up line shell by 108º Infantry Brigade and on communication line to line two.	
ENGLEBELMER	7/7/16	—	MESNIL section open to ENGLEBELMER.	
MARTINSART	7/7/16	—	1 section moved from ENGLEBELMER to MARTINSART.	
ENGLEBELMER	8/7/16 to 12/7/16	—	Working on front line + support line open line by 108º Infantry Brigade & on R.W. line behind two.	
ENGLEBELMER	13/7/16	—	MARTINSART section moved back to ENGLEBELMER.	
"	14/7/16 to 19/7/16	—	Working on front line + support line & other line open by 108 Infantry Brigade & on O.W. line behind two.	
"	20/7/16	—	d/o d/o	
"	27/7/16	—	Hq + 3 sections moved to FORCEVILLE. 1 section moved to AVELUY WOOD.	
FORCEVILLE	28-29/7/16	—		
AVELUY	29/7/16	—	Working on camp ways north over ANCRE, R/W depot centres	
WOOD	30/7/16	—		
"	31/7/16	—	2nd section moved to AVELUY WOOD.	

122/FIELD Vol 71

Army Form C. 2118.

WAR DIARY
or
INTELLIGENCE SUMMARY.
(Erase heading not required.)

CONFIDENTIAL

WAR DIARY

OF

122ⁿᵈ Field Coy R.E.

From April 1ˢᵗ 1916 to April 30ᵗʰ 1916

Volume 7

Army Form C. 2118.

WAR DIARY
or
INTELLIGENCE SUMMARY.
(Erase heading not required.)

Instructions regarding War Diaries and Intelligence Summaries are contained in F. S. Regs., Part II and the Staff Manual respectively. Title pages will be prepared in manuscript.

Place	Date	Hour	Summary of Events and Information	Remarks and references to Appendices
FORCEVILLE	1-4/16	-	Headquarters & 2 sections at FORCEVILLE	ex
AVELUY	1-4/16	-	2 sections at AVELUY WOOD	ex
HEDAUVILLE	2-4/16	-	1 section moved from FORCEVILLE to HEDAUVILLE	ex
On above	3-4/16 to 8-4/16	-	2 sections at AVELUY making a Causeway across RIVER ANCRE. 1 section at AVELUY working on dug-outs for R.A. 1 section at FORCEVILLE Bath and repair Carts.	ex
MARTINSART	9-4/16	-	1 section moved from FORCEVILLE to MARTINSART WOOD	ex
FORCEVILLE	10-4/16	-	Heavy rainfall & Small detachment from sections assisting under I.O. at FORCEVILLE	ex
AVELUY	to	-	Section 1 and 3 in AVELUY WOOD - Working at causeways across river Ancre for transport also of guns and in loading places for infantry.	ex
MARTINSART	30-4/16	-	Section No 4. Working at Div. Repair Cable at FORCEVILLE - MARTINSART ROAD	
HEDAUVILLE		-	Section No 2 working at dugout for R.A at HEDAUVILLE, also at dug out at HEDAUVILLE and on Dump post for ARMY - M.T. HEDAUVILLE.	

Vance
Maj i/c CE
OC 128th Field Coy CE

#353 Wt. W3544/1454 700,000 5/15 D. D. & L. A.D.S.S./Forms/C. 2118.

122 FᴱRᴱ MAY / Vol 8

WAR DIARY
or
INTELLIGENCE SUMMARY.

XXXVI

CONFIDENTIAL

WAR DIARY.
— of —
122ⁿᵈ Field Company RE

Period. May 1ˢᵗ 1916 to May 31ˢᵗ 1916

— Volume 8 —

Army Form C. 2118.

WAR DIARY
or
INTELLIGENCE SUMMARY.
(Erase heading not required.)

Instructions regarding War Diaries and Intelligence Summaries are contained in F. S. Regs., Part II. and the Staff Manual respectively. Title pages will be prepared in manuscript.

Place	Date	Hour	Summary of Events and Information	Remarks and references to Appendices
FORCEVILLE	1/7/16	10 P.M.	Headquarters and carpenters from Eastern Quarry works Dept and marking structures for the forward defences being constructed by the forward sections.	
AVELUY WOOD	1/5/16 to 10/7/16	5 P.M.	Sections 1 and 3 working at the erection of the new ANCRE north of AUTHUILLE, erecting 2 causeways to take guns or infantry in front and 7 crossing places for infantry in file.	
HESNIL	1/5/16 to 10/7/16	5 P.M.	No 2 section working at Div. OP and Army Survey Post - Nr. HESNIL, also at Div. Bomb Store & Div Ration Store near HARTINSART.	
HARTINSART WOOD	1/5/16 to 5/7/16	5 P.M.	No 4 section working at Div: Report Centre, & battle posts for 36 Div Staff or single shelter to 2 pill-boxes HARTINSART road	
	10/5/16	—	Section 3 moved to HARTINSART WOOD and erected 4 shelters to AVELUY WOOD delivering one another or ther posts.	
FORCEVILLE	11/5/16 to 30/5/16	—	Headquarters & carpenters from sections running workshop.	
AVELUY WOOD	11/5/16 to 31/5/16	—	Section 1 and 4 working at crossings of River ANCRE above AUTHUILLE.	
HESNIL	11/5/16 to 30/5/16	—	Section 2 working at Div OP and Army Survey Post and at Div Ration and Bomb Store.	
HARTINSART WOOD	11/5/16 to 30/5/16	—	Section 3 working at Div: Report Centre.	
—	31/5/16	—	Headquarters & carpenters from sections moved FORCEVILLE to HARTINSART and that workshop at latter place.	
—	31/5/16	—	No 2 section moved HESNIL to THIEPVAL WOOD to work on front line work there	

Murrill
Major RE

36th Divisional Engineers

122nd FIELD COMPANY R. E.

JUNE 1916

Army Form C. 2118.

WAR DIARY
or
INTELLIGENCE SUMMARY.

(Erase heading not required.)

June
122. FERE
XXXVI
Vol 9

CONFIDENTIAL

WAR DIARY

OF

122nd Field Company R.E.

Period. June 1st 1916 to June 30th 1916.

Volume 9.

Army Form C. 2118.

WAR DIARY
or
INTELLIGENCE SUMMARY.
(Erase heading not required.)

Page 1

Place	Date	Hour	Summary of Events and Information	Remarks and references to Appendices
MARTINSART	1/8 to 22/8	—	Ammunition and N°3 lecture. E/the engaged on Div Rgnl centre. Div Bomb Stores. Div Bomb OP. Army Rwy pier &c.	
AVELUY WOOD	1/8 to 20/8	—	Section 1 and 4? engaged on the causeway and entrance of the R. Ancre all month to make bridges and guns to be got across to THIEPVAL WOOD – also engaged on HQ emplacements in the front line of THIEPVAL WOOD	
THIEPVAL WOOD				
MOUND KEEP	23/8	—	3 sections of 106 to flow by Ancre to arrive in the Ancre evening. All 4 sections move to MOUND KEEP Q.35.B.30. – Sections engaged in constructing "Killos" for themselves. This is T day, and 5 days bombardment starts tomorrow. We have chosen 5 days from Zelero for V.W. X.Y and Z days.	
do	24/8	—	U day. – Bombardment of from our sections "killos". 1 aus Lt engaged in patrolling outskirts of the ANCRE between AUTHUILLE and Q24.C.54 and repairing damage caused by enemy "shells".	
do	25/8	—	V day – Bombardment continuing. Aug Sbourhood of MOUND KEEP heavily shelled by Germans on night 25/26 – one direct hit on a "Killo", one man injured.	
do	26/8	—	W day – 3rd day of bombardment – MOUND KEEP again shelled on night 26/27. no casualties.	
do	27/8	—	X day – 4 day of Bombardment.	

Army Form C. 2118.

WAR DIARY
or
INTELLIGENCE SUMMARY.

Page 2

(Erase heading not required.)

Place	Date	Hour	Summary of Events and Information	Remarks and references to Appendices
MOUND KERR?	28th	—	Y day - 5th day of bombardment - Bn. 110 Coy attacking with 108th Bgde is 9 R.IF. + 12th R.I.R. on left sector, and 11th, 13th & 15th R.I.R. right sector. BANGALORE TORPEDOES that we have near for them - left 2 extra drums 28 - 6'0" tubes 2 per coy in attack, right sector drum 28 tubes - 2 per coy in attack - Arm. informed that attack to proceed.	
	29th	—	11 day - 6th day of bombardment.	
	30th	—	12 day - 7 day of bombardment. At 10.0 PM No 3 section moves into HAMEL to accompany left sector of attack - No 2 section moves to THIEPVAL WOOD to accompany right sector of attack of 108th Bgde etc - Thos to come date Germans position when captured - Sappers details of left sector and 4 to right sector to attempt take charge of German positions. These two sections in Divisional reserve - Three (?) also to BANGALORE TORPEDOE parties.	

[signatures]

36th Divisional Engineers

122nd FIELD COMPANY R. E.

JULY 1916::

36/ Army Form C. 2118.

122 F C R E

Vol 10

WAR DIARY
or
INTELLIGENCE SUMMARY.

(Erase heading not required.)

Instructions regarding War Diaries and Intelligence Summaries are contained in F. S. Regs., Part II. and the Staff Manual respectively. Title pages will be prepared in manuscript.

Place	Date	Hour	Summary of Events and Information	Remarks and references to Appendices

CONFIDENTIAL

WAR DIARY
of
122 Field Coy R.E.

From 1st July 1916 to 31st July 1916.

Volume 10

G.H. Boam
Capt RE
for OC 122 Fd Coy RE
2/8/16

WAR DIARY or INTELLIGENCE SUMMARY.

Army Form C. 2118.

Place	Date	Hour	Summary of Events and Information	Remarks and references to Appendices
Martinsart MOUND KEEP (R.35.b.5.1.)	1/7/16		2 sections of Coy at MOUND KEEP in Div. Reserve. 2 sections with 108th Bgde = (1 in HAMEL subsector, 1 in Thiepval sub sector). These two sections were under orders of sub-sector commanders & were to be employed in consolidating enemy positions when taken & held. They were never employed in this work as the enemy position, though taken in the THIEPVAL subsector, was never really held – the sections were consequently never called on for this work by the Sub-sector Commanders. The section in the THIEPVAL subsector remained in assembly trenches – until recalled on the afternoon of the 1st except for some hours on the afternoon of the 1st when they were called upon to man the 2nd subsector under Lieut YOUNG was called upon to assist in holding the front line. The section in the HAMEL subsector under Lieut YOUNG of the second was continually employed on the afternoon of the 1st for some hours & from the evening of the 1st until the afternoon of the 2nd in unremitting work in evacuating wounded from this sector. Section in Divisional Reserve. Instructions received to send a section to repair railway crossing HAMEL northwards.	
	2/7/16	8.10 am	and also clear road from HAMEL towards BEAUCOURT STATION. 11 Lt. FARGHER & No 4 Section with material was detailed for this work. Near HAMEL railway crossing this section encountered a heavy artillery barrage on railway – on account of this & as RAILWAY SAP was still held by the enemy this section was ordered to withdraw & report to C.O. 9th R.I.Rif. 7 Coy. The section was employed evacuating wounded until finally withdrawn on the back at night. Orders received on night of 1st–2nd to send a section to THIEPVAL WOOD to clear it of German prisoners – No 1 section under C.S.M. Russell detailed. This section remained in THIEPVAL WOOD until 4 a.m. on the morning of the 2nd – but no prisoners were found. When returned to MOUND KEEP. Instructions received to recce MOUND KEEP & withdraw to AVELUY WOOD. This was carried out about 9.30 a.m. Instructions received to send all available men to report 107th Bgde. Capt. WIDDOWS & No 1 Section instructed by Division to commence sap from Top of ELGIN AV. across no mans land. This order was cancelled on representing the little progress that could be made in a day. Then instructed to carry consolidating material down to enemy trenches – prevented from doing this by enemy artillery barrage. After standing bye until 5.30 p.m. section was withdrawn by orders of Brigade. No 2 section withdrawn from THIEPVAL subsector, No 3 from HAMEL subsector & No 4 from same subsector afternoon of 2nd. Evening of second No 2&3 sections withdrawn to MARTINSART when No 1 section joined them later. No 4 section transferred to 121st Field Coy R.E. then at MOUND KEEP. Company moved to FORCEVILLE where it was joined by Transport details from Bivouac.	
	3/7/16		No 4 section rejoined Company from 121st Field Coy R.E.	
	7/7/16		" " FORCEVILLE to PUCHEVILLERS	
	9/7/16		" " PUCHEVILLERS to GEZAINCOURT	
	10/7/16		" " GEZAINCOURT via WARLINCOURT NEUVILLETTE to FREVENT where it entrained	
	11/7/16			
	12/7/16		Carried STEENBECQUE and marched to CAMPAGNE on night of 11th–12th July.	

Army Form C. 2118.

WAR DIARY
or
INTELLIGENCE SUMMARY.
(Erase heading not required.)

Instructions regarding War Diaries and Intelligence Summaries are contained in F. S. Regs., Part II. and the Staff Manual respectively. Title pages will be prepared in manuscript.

Place	Date	Hour	Summary of Events and Information	Remarks and references to Appendices
	13/7/16		Marched from CAMPAGNE to SERQUES	
	13/7/16 to 20/7/16		Remained at SERQUES refitting & refilling.	
	21/7/16		Marched to LEDRINGHEM from SERQUES.	
	22/7/16		" from LEDRINGHEM to WATOU.	
	24/7/16		" WATOU to CROIX DE POPERINGHE	
	25/7/16		" CROIX DE POPERINGHE to NEUVE EGLISE (Bulford Camp.)	
	27/7/16		Moved from Bulford Camp. H.Q. Transport, Horses etc to Aldershot Camp NEUVE EGLISE (T 13 B 7.2) 4 sections	
	27/7/16 to 31/7/16		to RED LODGE. (T 15 A 6.5.). One section detailed for work with Brigade in the line, 3 sections on M.G. emplacements on E of Hill 63 & front line	

G.M. Aldous
Capt. for Major R.E.
O.C. 122 Field Coy R.E.
2/8/16.

Vol II

CONFIDENTIAL

WAR DIARY

OF

122nd Field Coy RE

From August 1st 1916 to August 31st 1916

— Volume II —

WAR DIARY or INTELLIGENCE SUMMARY

Army Form C. 2118.

(Erase heading not required.)

Instructions regarding War Diaries and Intelligence Summaries are contained in F. S. Regs., Part II. and the Staff Manual respectively. Title pages will be prepared in manuscript.

Places	Date	Hour	Summary of Events and Information	Remarks and references to Appendices
RED LODGE	1/8 to 7/8	—	Four sections of Company at RED LODGE (TR A 65) N of PLOEGSTEERT. Transport and Headquarters below at ALDERSHOT CAMP T19 B 72 near NEUVE EGLISE. Sections working at H.Q. Supply dumps and Brigade Headquarters in 108th Infantry Brigade area. Section working for Brigade.	
"	8/8 to 12/8	—	Work as above. Supply dumps in course of construction are being re-sited in rather ammunition safer lines with an object of concrete walls with an apron and concrete roofs. Battalion Headquarters are to provide for the water surface and water of their timing existing buildings by new concrete walls and roofs.	
	13/8 to		3 sections continuing on above work. Section above the trenches are starting on making extra dug-outs in the front line. This consists of a shelter piece of five trench, little to give a good command and having a gas proof and to entrance and installing gas proof shelters built. The gas proof paradox and so water to both to hour to hour. The water being first to water the live can be kept by three pounds only.	
	20/8 21/8 to 6/31/8		Work of the 4 sections continuing as above —	

Signed [signature]
MAJOR, R.E.
O.C. 122ND. FIELD COY. R.E.

Army Form C. 2118.

Vol 12

WAR DIARY
or
INTELLIGENCE SUMMARY.
(Erase heading not required.)

CONFIDENTIAL

WAR DIARY

OF

122 FIELD COMPANY R.E.

From 1st September 1916 to 30th September 1916.

VOLUME 12

Army Form C. 2118.

WAR DIARY
or
INTELLIGENCE SUMMARY.
(Erase heading not required.)

Instructions regarding War Diaries and Intelligence
Summaries are contained in F. S. Regs., Part II.
and the Staff Manual respectively. Title pages
will be prepared in manuscript.

Place	Date	Hour	Summary of Events and Information	Remarks and references to Appendices
Red Lodge	1/9/16 to 7/9/16	—	Four sections of Company at RED LODGE (T.18 d 65) N. of PLOEGSTEERT Headquarters Section & transport at ALDERSHOT CAMP. (T.19 b 73) near NEUVE EGLISE (as in last month War Diary) 3 sections working on M.G. emplacements in 108th Bgde area under the Division — 1 section working on Brigade work (Front line Dugouts, strong points etc.) as in last month War Diary	
	8/9/16	—	Headquarters section & transport moved from ALDERSHOT CAMP to LE ROMARIN. Map referred B4 & 73 on "France Sheet 36 N.W. 1/20,000	
	9/9/16 to 25/9/16	—	Work continued as above	
	26/9/16 to 28/9/16	—	100 Boxes to contain 200 gas cylinders were installed in Trenches 135, 136 & 137 by the section on Brigade work with the assistance of one of the sections from Divisional Work	
	29/9/16 30/9/16	—	Work on M.G. Emplacements & Battalion HQ. by three sections & ordinary Brigade work by one section resumed.	

[signature]
MAJOR, R.E.
O.C. 122ND. FIELD COY. R.E.

Vol 13

CONFIDENTIAL -

WAR DIARY

OF

- 122nd Field Coy RE - 36th Division

From. October 1st 1916 to October 31st 1916.

Volume 13 -

Army Form C. 2118.

WAR DIARY
or
INTELLIGENCE SUMMARY.
(Erase heading not required.)

Instructions regarding War Diaries and Intelligence Summaries are contained in F. S. Regs., Part II. and the Staff Manual respectively. Title pages will be prepared in manuscript.

Place	Date	Hour	Summary of Events and Information	Remarks and references to Appendices
RED LODGE	1/7/16	—	Two sections of Company at RED LODGE. T.16.D.65. N.Z. PLOEGSTEERT	
LE ROMARIN	to	—	Headquarters, cookers and transport at LE ROMARIN. O.4.473. in France Kent 28 m/m 1/50,000	
RED LODGE	3/7/16	—	Took over cables and in wires of Coy held by the 108th Coy/Sanitary Brigade	
PETIT POINT FARM	4/7/16	—	Two sections moved into billets at PETIT POINT FARM. T.22.B.12. White of RED LODGE being taken over by 7th Brigade.	
"	"	—	Sections continuing to work in this area covered tracing over the formation of a new support line, concrete M.G. emplacement and dugouts, and battalion and company headquarters.	
"	"	—	Drainage in this area (in rear of the RIVER DOUVE) is difficult. The Coy. borrow ans the STEENEBEEK was especially. with heavy rain flooding approaches trenches and dugouts. Since these R.E. have been cleared out the curves have been constantly clear.	
"	3/7/16	—	One "fish" by 4.2" HE Shells however for an objects earth stopped conjure with a 12" shell of unfired amount and on a surface conjunct MG emplacement. Both the line at its three walls & ait so a lentils and with instructions to illuminate In the front further causing it showed of an as affair to illustrate and confirm conjuring although occupants escaped injury. In the lutter case where entrances were favoured no structural damage occurred	

2353 Wt. W3544/1454 700,000 5/15 D.D. & L. A.D.S.S./Forms/C. 2118.

[Signed] MAJOR, R.E.
O.C. 122ND. FIELD COY. R.E.

Vol 14

- Confidential -
- War Diary -
of
122nd Field Company R.E. 26 Division

From November 1st 1916 to November 30th 1916

Volume 14 -

Confidential
Army Form C. 2118.

WAR DIARY
or
INTELLIGENCE SUMMARY.
(Erase heading not required.)

122nd Field Coy R.E.

Instructions regarding War Diaries and Intelligence Summaries are contained in F.S. Regs., Part II. and the Staff Manual respectively. Title pages will be prepared in manuscript.

Place	Date	Hour	Summary of Events and Information	Remarks and references to Appendices
Petit Pont	1/8	—	HEADQUARTERS BILLETS at PETIT PONT T.22.B.1.2	
Le Romarin	1/8	—	Headquarters transport at LE ROMARIN B.4.9.73. Limits Nos 35 MM 12 loads.	
Petit Pont	1/8 6-7/8	—	Relieving working in area occupied by 189th Infantry Brigade. Working mainly on New Support line. The construction of a new trench from B Gurkha Redoubt T.5.D.23 to Ration Farm T.12.A.9.51. dugouts for company in support. New communication trenches TM emplacements etc.	
"	7/8	—	Following very heavy rains the River Douve rose about 8 feet so the night of 7-8/8. Flooding ground east side of the River.	
"	8/8	—	Work continuing in this area. Revetting of the Front line with A frames being necessary as trench works were giving way badly in many places.	
"	6-30/8	—	Very little hostile activity, especially at night, and enemy. I used low Pine for in working night work and night carrying much easier than usual. Considerable trench mortar activity on our part, but very little retaliation by enemy and in consequence very few repairs to trenches from damage by shell fire, required.	

M. Churchill
Major R.E.
O.C. 122 Field Coy R.E.

Confidential

WAR DIARY
of
122nd Field Company R.E.

36th Division

From December 1st 1916 to December 21st 1916.

Volume 15

WAR DIARY or INTELLIGENCE SUMMARY

Army Form C. 2118.

Place	Date	Hour	Summary of Events and Information	Remarks and references to Appendices
PETIT PONT.	1/9/16	—	4 Lectures billeted at PETIT PONT T.22.B.12	(B)
LE ROMARIN	1/9/16		Heavy hostile visitors and transport at LE ROMARIN B.4.A.7.3. Enemy shell 38 MV. '20.000	(B)
PETIT PONT to 29/9/16			Lectures working in area occupied by 106th Infantry Brigade working mainly on the following — New Support Line (HANBURY NORTH) U.1.D.0040 to U.12.C.58 — now transverse from ST QUENTIN CABARET T.5.D.23 to PATRON FARM T.2.A.51. — dugouts for snipers area in support FORT OSBORNE BARRACKS. U.12.C.1545 and WELL LANE U.7.B.58 — New communication trenches T.H. emplacements etc. Calgary Avenue completion through to front line T.6.C.62 to U.1.D.48 — Considerable increase in hostile artillery fire, in particular WELL LANE U.7.B.55. CURRIE AV EAST U.7.B.69 to U.2.C.22, our front line in U.2.C, reportedly knocked in, and requiring considerable amount of repair.	(B)
PETIT PONT	30/9/16	—	As 106th Brigade moved out of this Bn on rest on supt. 29/30, work in this area handed over to 12th and 150th Fus Bdes. 12th Bn working in area NJ Calgary avenue, and 150th Bn working in area S.J. this 129th Bn remaining at PETIT PONT and engaged in Front area 1/10	(B)

N.B. unless otherwise stated map references are from PLOEGSTEERT, edition 3.D. 28.SW.4.

Vol 16

CONFIDENTIAL

WAR DIARY

OF

122nd Field Company R.E.

36th Division

From January 1st 1917 to January 31st 1917

Volume 16

Army Form C. 2118.

WAR DIARY
INTELLIGENCE SUMMARY.
(Erase heading not required.)

Instructions regarding War Diaries and Intelligence Summaries are contained in F.S. Regs., Part II. and the Staff Manual respectively. Title pages will be prepared in manuscript.

Place	Date	Hour	Summary of Events and Information	Remarks and references to Appendices
Petit Pont	1/7		4 sections at Petit Pont (T 22 B 12) H.Q. section and Transport at Le Romarin (B 4 a 73 – France sheet 36 NW 1/20,000) Company engaged on following work – PALMER BATHS (Neuve Eglise) running & maintenance – Increasing Drying accomodation. DRANOUTRE BATHS – Running & maintenance – improvement of Drying hooms – erection of shed for Tailors & being Regd. Decorators. HYDE PARK CORNER. (U 19 b 35½) Running Electric lighting installation & following "t" [?] consisting 1 Gas petrol motor driven generator approximately 5 Kilowatts 220 volts – one set being fixed by Improving Installation & running new wiring. Hill 63. Repairs & Improvements to Forts, running round them. 18. Ur Gun position at T 23 b 35 for six guns. 2 gun position for 4.5 Howitzers at U 19 b 59. Construction 1 wooden Tramway for artillery Battery in T 17. Red Lodge – Dugouts at TT 18 0954 obtained & improved. Subsidiary Line on Hill 63. New wire intrenchments.	[initials]
	26/7		These are the most important works – Company employed on general work in back Divisional area. Company hard from Petit Pont & Romarin to Branders: Monmouthshire Camp & Kurzan Camp & Tent hut work in forward area system of works Left Brigade area of Divisional Front. Work done taken over from the 131st Field Coy. R.E. (Unless otherwise stated Map references are from PLOEGSTEERT sheet 28 SW/4 edition 3D. 1/20000)	[initials]

O.C. 172nd FIELD COY. R.E.

3353 Wt. W3544/1454 700,000 5/15 D.D. & L. A.D.S.S./Forms/C. 2118.

CONFIDENTIAL

Army Form C. 2118.

WAR DIARY

~~INTELLIGENCE SUMMARY.~~

(Erase heading not required.)

Instructions regarding War Diaries and Intelligence Summaries are contained in F.S. Regs., Part II. and the Staff Manual respectively. Title pages will be prepared in manuscript.

Vol 17

Summary of Events and Information

OF

122nd Field Company R.E.

36th Division

From February 1st 1917 to February 28th 1917

VOLUME 17

[Stamp: 122ND COY. ROYAL ENGINEERS * ULSTER DIVISION * No. a/124 Date 1-3-1917]

Place	Date	Hour		Remarks and references to Appendices

Army Form C. 2118.

WAR DIARY
or
INTELLIGENCE SUMMARY.

(Erase heading not required.)

Instructions regarding War Diaries and Intelligence Summaries are contained in F. S. Regs., Part II. and the Staff Manual respectively. Title pages will be prepared in manuscript.

Place	Date	Hour	Summary of Events and Information	Remarks and references to Appendices
Draincourt	1/2/17	—	Company located at Draincourt - Monmouth Camp & Lugan Camp & working in left Bydr area of Divisional front - one section on front line work - a one section working behind front line in each subsection. One section on Divisional work.	2/w
	5/2/17	—	One section - the one on front line work - moved from Draincourt to DE KENNEBAK (T 3 b 2 o). Rest of Company remain at Draincourt.	2/w
	14/2/17	—	Two Sections moved from Draincourt to Neuve Eglise (T 15 a 32) & one section moved from DE Kennebak to Neuve Eglise. Headquarters of Company now at Neuve Eglise (T 15 a 32). Section on Divisional work & hagan line remains at Draincourt.	2/w
	28/2/17	—	Distribution - 1 Company remain as 14/2/17	

W. Mount
Capt R.E. for Major R.E.
O.C. 122 Field Coy

Army Form C. 2118.

WAR DIARY
or
INTELLIGENCE SUMMARY.

(Erase heading not required.)

Vol 18

CONFIDENTIAL

WAR DIARY

OF

122nd FIELD COMPANY R.E.

36th DIVISION

From March 1st 1917 to March 31st 1917

Volume 18

Army Form C. 2118.

WAR DIARY
or
INTELLIGENCE SUMMARY.
(Erase heading not required.)

Instructions regarding War Diaries and Intelligence Summaries are contained in F. S. Regs., Part II and the Staff Manual respectively. Title pages will be prepared in manuscript.

Place	Date	Hour	Summary of Events and Information	Remarks and references to Appendices
NEUVE EGLISE	1/7	—	Headquarters and 3 sections of company in billets in NEUVE EGLISE – House Lines and Reserve at MONMOUTH CAMP – DRANOUTRE. One section working on front line in centre sector. 4th section in general work.	(1)
	2/7 to 7/7	—	4th section moved from DRANOUTRE to NEUVE EGLISE – 2 sections working on behind front line in cent. centre & in right sector. Front line divided into 4 sections for work, each 1 section allotted to each section according to own front to man.	(2)
	8/7	—	4th section moved from DRANOUTRE to NEUVE EGLISE.	(3)
	9/7 to 13/7	—	Intense enemy bombardment on left of own line. Line by 12 R.I.R. and on line of 16th Division on our left during afternoon. Much damage done to our front line and subs of comn. trenches. Two to three sections put on at 9.0pm and worked up to line to repair damage – worked till 3.0am when front line and communication line were more permanent. Three hours were caused by enemy against our front about 4.0 a.m. Company did trench bath on relief	(4)
	14/7	—		(5)
	15/7	—	1 unit in the area handed over to 2nd New Zealand Field Company, who took over line from our Coy. Brigade (106th Brigade). 2 sections moved to billets behind LINDENHOEK. Headquarters and 2 sections moved to LOCRE. The fourth moved with four coys of 16th Division over 107th Brigade as taking over from a Brigade of 16th Division, our Division leaving our Brigade in the line.	(6)
	17/7	—	Headquarters moved to billets behind LINDENHOEK. 2 other sections moved to billets behind LINDENHOEK. Four lines training at DRANOUTRE.	(7)
	18/7 to 31/7	—	Company working on defensive and offensive work – at present work crossing of new M.G. emplacements, and belts of wire in subsidiary line, and on improving reserve line. Offensive preps working drawn up by own battalion battle lines training.	(8)

Signed [illegible], Major O.C.
O.C. 122nd New Ind. R.E.

Army Form C. 2118.

WAR DIARY
or
INTELLIGENCE SUMMARY.
(Erase heading not required.)

Vol 19

— CONFIDENTIAL —

— WAR DIARY —

OF

— 122ND FIELD COMPANY. R.E. —

— 36TH DIVISION. —

— FROM APRIL 1ST 1917 TO APRIL 30TH 1917 —

— VOLUME 19. —

Army Form C. 2118.

WAR DIARY
or
INTELLIGENCE SUMMARY.
(Erase heading not required.)

Instructions regarding War Diaries and Intelligence Summaries are contained in F.S. Regs., Part II and the Staff Manual respectively. Title pages will be prepared in manuscript.

Place	Date	Hour	Summary of Events and Information	Remarks and references to Appendices
LINDENHOEK	1/7	—	Headquarters and H section in billets behind LINDENHOEK. Two lines at MONMOUTH CAMP DRANOUTRE.	A
	1/7	—	Company working on both defensive & offensive work — defensive work consisting of N.S. improvements and billets of wire in ordinary line, and in improving the reserve line. Offensive preparation consisting of new battalion Headquarters in the left half sub sector.	A
	6/7	—	2 platoons moved to new camp at N26 A81.	A
	8/7	—	" " " " N26 A81.	A
	9/7	—	3rd section " " " "	
	10/7	—	Work started on new main up communication trench to left trigger the offensive. Also in rear of QUEENS GATE and new firm Bullis Farm to Font Line. Working parties on April 24th of 9th R. of Reg. 2 platoons on butt Reg. 1 on MG update. 2 on reserve trench. 2 on support with story (N.B) line. 1 on kitchery + 3 on Pueno Gate. Working parties from 10/7 they were come on the 70 trench for general training. Reserve parties of 7/6 R.M. Ref (P) employed in —	A
	14/7	—	New working parties available from 108th Brigade on their return from training employing on filant. 9 platoons 6 plat Pueno Gate. 1 on trench tramway. 1 on running store.	A
	20/7 to 29/7	—	Work concentrated on offensive preparation as opposed to use of defensive until two sections.	
	29/7	—	H section + Headquarters moved to N26 A81.	
	30/7	—	Army Helio NEHHE recently, but did not interfere with our work.	A

Army Form C. 2118.

WAR DIARY
or
INTELLIGENCE SUMMARY.
(Erase heading not required.)

Vol 20

Confidential

War Diary
of
122nd Field Coy RE
36th Div.
from 1/5/17 to 31/5/17

WAR DIARY or INTELLIGENCE SUMMARY

Army Form C. 2118.

Place	Date	Hour	Summary of Events and Information	Remarks and references to Appendices
LINDENHOEK	1/7	—	Headquarters and 4 sections in billets in KEMMEL HILL behind LINDENHOEK. Horse lines at MONMOUTH CAMP, DRANOUTRE.	A
	2/7	—	Company working on preparations for the offensive, and supplied with working parties for the 11th R.F. Rifles distributed as follows.	A
			1 platoon on new mainline communication trench QUEEN'S GATE. 1 platoon on improving old communication trenches REGENT STREET, PALL MALL. 2 platoons on french tramway system. 2 platoons on left Brigade battle battalion headquarters. 1 platoon on divisional Horse lines, and 1 platoon on running R.E. stores.	
	4/7	—	Started getting up R.E. stores into forward dumps for offensive. Started work on improving track from DRANOUTRE to LINDENHOEK as main road from DRANOUTRE to LINDENHOEK via DAYLIGHT CORNER is frequently shelled and new track provides good alternative route.	A
			Capt McILDOWIE goes to C.R.E. as adjutant. Lieut KERR turns 2nd in command of company. Started work on new R.A.P. for left brigade. Working parties supplied by R.A.M.C.	
	6/7	—	Capt GREENWOOD R.E. instructor at 2nd Army School arrived to be attached to this company for instruction in trench work for 6 days.	A
	7/7	—	Burrows at Horse Lines.	A
	11/7	—	Started work on water conservation in forward area, in unrolling tents and barrels and digging saveouts. Started work on filling in trenches which were over run, so as to enable transport to be got forward.	A

WAR DIARY
or
INTELLIGENCE SUMMARY.
(Erase heading not required.)

Army Form C. 2118.

Place	Date	Hour	Summary of Events and Information	Remarks and references to Appendices
	11/7	-	Extending the metre gauge line between KEMMEL and DAYLIGHT corner into 60 cm.	
	12/7	-	improving existing tramway system and laying new laterals.	
	13/7	-	Italian work on O.P.'s for gunners.	
	14/7	-	Working parties of 11th R.S.F. & I. Torpst as 108th Inf Bde are going into line, and 109 Inf Brigade coming out into Divisional Reserve.	
	16/7	-	Working parties supplied from 11th R. Innis Fus. 11 platoons.	
	20/7	-	100 infantry attached to this company. 25 from each battalion in 108th Brig area.	
	22/7	-	Company F Foot Irish Pioneers 11th Division working under this company on tramway work. They will work with Dy Balch Torrens after the attack working under Type but in meantime will work with us on general tramway work to obtain in reserve.	
	23/7	-	Marked out overland routes in left Brigade area.	
	24/7	-	Newshooting shooting in way of our artillery fire and felling trees.	
	28/7	-	C.R.E. 36 Division killed by shell at Dickebusch. Kruisstraete. Bore to caving a 13 c.m. gun known as "whistling Percy" - some falling near this camp, majority further from tramway DRANOUTRE.	
			M.G. Coy 32nd Brig use 11th Division working in line making M.G barrage	
	31/7	-	In the slow. Sapper being trained in their spare time in use of bombs, bayonet and Lewis gun, a supper are exposed to continuous rain and worked up to a slow without much change of any young training. Old artillery fire pretty heavy work practically complete.	

A.D.S.S./Forms/C. 2118.

O.C. 122nd FIELD COY. R.E.

Army Form C. 2118.

WAR DIARY
or
INTELLIGENCE SUMMARY.
(Erase heading not required.)

Vol 21

WAR DIARY

OF

122nd FIELD COMPANY R.E.

FROM

June 1st 1917 to June 30th 1917.

VOLUME 21.

Army Form C. 2118.

WAR DIARY
or
INTELLIGENCE SUMMARY.
(Erase heading not required.)

Instructions regarding War Diaries and Intelligence Summaries are contained in F.S. Regs., Part II. and the Staff Manual respectively. Title pages will be prepared in manuscript.

Place	Date	Hour	Summary of Events and Information	Remarks and references to Appendices
HAPPY VALLEY CAMP. 28.S.W. 26.A.7.1.	1/6/17	"	Headquarters and HEctions at Happy Valley Camp – Horse lines at MONMOUTH CAMP, DRANOUTRE. Work in connection with offensive preparations practically complete, both Brigade & battalion Inspections finished. Spent about C.O.'s finished. Surveyed horse lines. Reported sick for tramway to finished. Instructed in the probable tasks for the offensive, 2 field companies to consolidate strong points in 2nd and 4th objective known as BLUE and BLACK lines and 122nd coy to wire the fourth objective of 36th Division (BLACK LINE) Making forward dumps for 1st Brigade and for battalions of Left Brigade. Brigade dump at N29C4Y. Batt Dumps:- 1st N29A4.9. – 1st N29A25 – 2st N29C.7.Y. all strips in three dumps being made up into new bags.	
do.	2/6/17	"	Making forward dumps for 122nd coy. 1 for left Half company at N29A5Y, 1 for right half company of Coy & medium trench mortars for right half company at N29C9Y. These dumps consisting of I.T.M. and Small Arms Ammunition wire and barbed wire all made up into mats wire and wire trans. Extra mule trans made up at Happy Valley Camp and spontoons wagons bread up and with 100 man loads of sandbags, barbed wire and covered pickets respectively.	
do.	4/6/17	"	Sappers being instructed daily in wiring drill.	

Army Form C. 2118.

WAR DIARY
or
INTELLIGENCE SUMMARY.
(Erase heading not required.)

Place	Date	Hour	Summary of Events and Information	Remarks and references to Appendices
HAPPY VALLEY CAMP.	5/7/17		In accordance with instructions from CRE- 1 Junior NCO and 20% of each section selected to be left behind.	
	6/7/17		20% to be left behind sent to MONMOUTH Camp DARTMOUTHE. Happy Valley Camp struck. 3 Officers & 150 O. Ray mounted — Lieut Montgomery & Lieut J. Thos company proceeded at 3.30 P.M.	
	7/7/17		Mules went up & taking camp - Company paraded at 8.0 A.M. Company order without packs, now strength to stand by - . 12 mules arrived from Brigade at 8.0 A.M. starting 20 in all with our own company pack mules. Paraded at Happy Valley. — O.C. company — 4 R.E. lectures at 80% strength, sent with R.E. Lecture officer. — 100 Blacks infantry from 108th Brigade, 25 non R.E. Lectures and l attached infantry officer — 8 Field company mules with drivers — 12 attached mules from infantry brigade with drivers — 2 R.E. mounted N.C.O.s —	
		4.0 P.M.	Received orders from CRE that company would go up and view the BLACK LINE. Mules travel up at Happy Valley and company moved off in 2 half companies to dumps at N29A.57 and N29C.97. — O.C. with one half company and attached infantry officer with other half company, each half company having 10 pack mules with it & 1 mounted NCO (Chaumont)	

2353 Wt. W2544/1454 700,000 5/15 D. D. & L. A.D.S.S. Forms/C. 2118.

WAR DIARY
or
INTELLIGENCE SUMMARY.
(Erase heading not required.)

Army Form C. 2118.

Place	Date	Hour	Summary of Events and Information	Remarks and references to Appendices
	7/6/17	—	On arrival at 2 Company dumps each RE and Infantry picket up a man load, and Inf Companys moved up to BLACK LINE & relieving S.F.J. O20c and O26 central. Men and mule loads carried over as follows – Thus for the men are on the top of line but allowance was made for the very long carry (over 2500 yards) and for the fact that Support had to move on arrival and infantry would have to move a second time. __Men loads__: – The Chinnii (?crew) pickets – 4 in bundle for carrying on shoulder – 6 in 2 packs/bags. The months of the sandbags sewn together and the 2 bags hanging front & rear of man. 8 on a Yukon pack. 3 in a bundle. __Long (?crew) pickets__ – 2 men to carry (⅓ of large size) tied twisted n/6 Figure of eight, rest over and used together. __Barbed wire__ – One coil on a stave. __Mule loads__. __Barbed wire__ – 5 coils. 2 on a long stave on either side and one on top of saddle in the middle. __Long (?crew) pickets__ + Barbed wire – 20 pickets and 1 coil of barbed wire – pickets in 2 sandbag-wrapped bundles of 10 each, slung on each side of mule. Front end of bundle being kept up by stave rest out. Barbed wire in centre of saddle	

A.D.S.S. Forms/C. 2118

WAR DIARY or INTELLIGENCE SUMMARY

Army Form C. 2118.

Place	Date	Hour	Summary of Events and Information	Remarks and references to Appendices
	6/7/17		Total front to be wired by the Company was 1200 yds. ie 300 yds per section, and for a couple entanglement consisting of 1 row long row pickets, 2 rows medium pickets, 3 long and 1 row on each row of pickets and one set of chequered pickets 9' spacing and 9' between rows of pickets. 9 wires for each 300 yds of entanglement - 100 long pickets, 100 medium pickets and 20 coils of wire. This would be carried up as follows:-	

Per section.

	Trepieds	Med. pickets	Long pickets
1st Run - RE. 10 men each with 6 medium pickets	-	60	-
15 " " " 3 long	45	-	-
Infantry. 6 ytons " " 8 medium	-	48	-
14 men " "	-	-	14
Mules. 2 each with 5 coils	-	-	10
3 " " 20 trepieds + 1 coil.	60	-	3
	105	108	27

ie 1st run if all got to site would make the complete entanglement and 2nd run would improve it.

7 PM North Staff. Company arrived at BLACK LINE at 10 PM and covering

WAR DIARY
or
INTELLIGENCE SUMMARY.

Army Form C. 2118.

Place	Date	Hour	Summary of Events and Information	Remarks and references to Appendices
	7/7		Started at once, wire being started about 40 yds in front of French line laid by the infantry and joining up with 16th Division on left flank, near STEENYZER CAB. at O.20.C.4.4 and with 25th Division on the right flank at LUMM FARM. (O.26.D.3.8) On arrival at BLACK LINE, 3 German R.E. dumps were found at O.26.A.5.6, O.20.C.25.20 and O.20.A.3.1, these contained barbed wire, barbed wire concertinas and screw pickets, and wire and infantry were utilised in carrying forward these dumps to BLACK LINE, mules being used took some time before stock, so that drivers could have had a day back.	B.
	"	12.0 midnight	By midnight a complete belt of wire of a minimum width of 18 feet and tramway for a considerable length had been completed and company moved back to Happy Valley Camp.	
HAPPY VALLEY CAMP	8/7	6.0 p.m.	Company left Happy Valley Camp at 6.0 p.m. in same formation as night before with 12 mules. These mules were broken up at left company pioneer dump and were moved up by lift. A word of any kind between Pioneer Dump and front, and with a 5 yard	S.

Army Form C. 2118.

WAR DIARY
or
INTELLIGENCE SUMMARY.
(Erase heading not required.)

Instructions regarding War Diaries and Intelligence Summaries are contained in F. S. Regs., Part II. and the Staff Manual respectively. Title pages will be prepared in manuscript.

Place	Date	Hour	Summary of Events and Information	Remarks and references to Appendices
	8/6	—	Between the Sentry towards was commenced in front of the BLACK LINE	
		9.30 PM	A tactile bombardment started and we started barrage fire, the 123rd company with attached infantry accordingly stood to in the BLACK LINE with the infantry the from 9.30 PM to 11.0 PM. — at 11.0 PM things quietened down and work was resumed, the 2nd infantry company being completed the wire ing th of the Black Line and of a minimum breadth of 9 feet.	S
DRANOUTRE	9/6	—	123rd Bty and attached infantry marched back to DRANOUTRE. A company of the 11th Division taking over Happy Valley Camp.	S
	10/6	—	Attached infantry rejoin their battalions	S
N 25 D 21.	13/6	—	Attached infantry rejoin the company and attached infantry moved to sub bivouac at N 25 D 21. Horse lines run among the ?? in front of the BLACK LINE working	S
	14/6	—	Company working at improving it a breadth of 100 yds. and infantry consisting of a screw of belts with fences between them.	
HAPPY VALLEY CAMP	19/6	—	Company and attached infantry moved to Happy Valley Camp taking over horse lines also moved from DRANOUTRE Horse lines also moved from DRANOUTRE	S

WAR DIARY or INTELLIGENCE SUMMARY

Army Form C. 2118.

Place	Date	Hour	Summary of Events and Information	Remarks and references to Appendices
HAPPY VALLEY CAMP	1917 June	—	to Happy Valley Camp. 38th Divn. were taking over the IX Corps front. Company working on wiring in front of the MAUVE LINE which is a line in front of the BLACK LINE.	
	19th to 24th		Company wiring in front of MAUVE LINE.	S
	25th		Company wiring — Capt YERR and Lieut Bruce went out to positions behind the OSTEAVERNE line, the 2 companies on either flank.	S
	26th		Company wiring. Eight German guns which had been abandoned in recent advance. Very heavy rain. Found some +3" howitzers in position afraid of access owing to sticken condition of ground. Reconnoitring for gun again in positions spotted by 11th Division. Found no guns except one tracked one. 11th Division men informs badly out. Twenty killed tonight - locally if front this morning very unhealthy.	S
	27th		Gun out numbers of 1.77mm gun. Out tonight S. Park — Found others but w/s too few been dismantled in end. These could not be removed before daylight.	S
	28th		Heavy thunderstorm prevented any more guns being taken.	S
	29th		Handed over work in touch to Field Company of 37th Divn. Attached wiring others to work.	S
	30th 4.0 AM		Company moved Hd to POPERINGHE and billeted there the night. 37th Divn. now are taking over line from 38th.	

T. Maurice
Major O.C.
122nd Field Coy R.E.

Army Form C. 2118.

WO 22

WAR DIARY
or
INTELLIGENCE SUMMARY.
(Erase heading not required.)

Confidential

War Diary
of
122nd Field Company, R.E.
from July 31st 1914
July 1st 1917 to

Volume 22

Army Form C. 2118.

WAR DIARY
or
INTELLIGENCE SUMMARY.
(Erase heading not required.)

Instructions regarding War Diaries and Intelligence Summaries are contained in F. S. Regs., Part II. and the Staff Manual respectively. Title pages will be prepared in manuscript.

Place	Date	Hour	Summary of Events and Information	Remarks and references to Appendices
POPERINGE	1/7/17		Company moved from POPERINGE to WINNEZEELE. Tents erected & horse lines made. No 2 Coy 16º Rl R. (Pioneers) arrived on detachment.	
WINNEZEELE	2/7/17		Sites for wells selected. Tool carts overhauled.	
"	3/7/17		Commenced work on wells. Wells shallow type approx 20' deep according to nature of ground, 5' genuine diameter with 2" straight edge forest planking 6"x3" collars 1"x3" stays. Wells covered supplied with lid, bucket & rope. Location bound & fenced round to keep TB cattle system of working three 8 hour shifts on each well.	
"	7/7/17		Earth augur used for boring as difficulty was found in locating water. A most useful & efficient tool. Four men in good ground could put down an 18' bore hole in 35 minutes.	
"	20/7/17		No 2 Coy. 16º Rl R rejoined their Battalion.	

Army Form C. 2118.

WAR DIARY
or
INTELLIGENCE SUMMARY.
(Erase heading not required.)

Place	Date	Hour	Summary of Events and Information	Remarks and references to Appendices
NINEZEELE	24/9/17		Major Hardie went on leave to England	
"	"		Took over 150 Field Coy's work. e.g. 3 wells or completion	
"	25"		9 New Nissen huts. No. 2 Coy. wells pegged in as no timber available to complete 18 wells completed.	
"	26" to 30"		Bath house erected, K8 horse troughs in No. 1, 2, & 3 areas erected. Two canvas reservoirs for water points erected complete with pumps. Pickets & hook put on wells. Company practised erecting Weldon trestles & did training suitable for Open Warfare. Route marches, extended order drill. 27/9/17 Lieut Morcomb	
	30"	10 P.M.	Coy. moved to L 16 A central (Sheet 27) Roads very bad. Advance party took tents (24)	went to Hospital
	31"	5 A.M.	Arrived L 16 A Central. Pontoons & trestles brought from WINNEZEELE	

Army Form C. 2118.

Vol 23

WAR DIARY
or
INTELLIGENCE SUMMARY.
(Erase heading not required.)

War Diary
of
122nd Field Coy. R.E.

from

1st August 1917 to 31st August 1917

Volume 23.

Army Form C. 2118.

WAR DIARY
or
INTELLIGENCE SUMMARY.
(Erase heading not required.)

Instructions regarding War Diaries and Intelligence Summaries are contained in F.S. Regs., Part II. and the Staff Manual respectively. Title pages will be prepared in manuscript.

Summary of Events and Information Map reference - Belgium 28 NW 1/20,000 unless otherwise mentioned

Place	Date	Hour	Summary of Events and Information	Remarks and references to Appendices
1.1.B.A Central sheet 27.	1/7/17		2 Company in bivouac in fields WEST of POPERINGHE. weather very wet.	B
	2/8/17		121st and 122nd Companies in the field near by.	B
	3/8/17		100 attached infantry from 108 & Bde. also 1 Bund company on 1.8.17.	B
	4/8/17		Company moved forward and took over billets and work of 425 Field Coy RE, 55th Division.	
YPRES.			122nd Company This location as follows:- Horse Lines and mounted transport and 10% of sappers from teatins at H.2.C.O.8. - Detachment on demand of R.E. dump at H.8.A.5.9. Headquarters and 4/10ths at J.19.A.18, and East of MENIN GATE, YPRES. (100 a Trailer infantry will return in from from killed) Company working on Tracks, one a vehicle track running from YPRES and running NORTH of and parallel to the main MENIN GATE - POTIJZE ROAD which it tube at about C.29.A.3.2. the Track (N.4) continuing EAST from here as a mule track, running up to Britan Front Line (known as BLACK LINE) which it reaches at about C.24.B.90.40. The other track being a duckboard track for men, starting from OXFORD ROAD at C.29.A.1.3 and running Eastward towards front line, keeping to the North of Track 4 (mule track) starting points available - A RE detains, 100 Trailed infantry over 100 infantry who were up by train every night.	B
	7/7/17		Kept RIGE and Sapper SKELLION killed at forward dumps, and 6 men wounded.	B
	8/8/17		Took over forward RE dump at POTIJZE from 121st Company.	B
	9/7/17		Started working forward dumps of RE material at where track 4 crosses OXFORD ROAD Battalions will draw from this to form then forward battalion dumps for the offensive, dumps also available for RE.	B

Army Form C. 2118.

WAR DIARY
or
INTELLIGENCE SUMMARY.
(Erase heading not required.)

Place	Date	Hour	Summary of Events and Information	Remarks and references to Appendices
YPRES.	10/8	-	Work continuing on trench. Hostile artillery very active, and parties are killed every day and night up to the job on the job, and on way back to billets. Neighbourhood of billets also is shelled pretty constantly. A good many casualties among RE and attached infantry. At night enemy are throwing over 9.2" shell in very large numbers, the effect of this is very local and unless our trench were near, if seems impossible to obtain a 9.2 concentration heavy enough to effect men. Men are very quick at putting the tops of their respirators into their mouths and we are trying as much cavalry from gas shell - thus few men are going sick with vomiting and diarrhoea caused by gas, but they do not seem seriously ill.	Q.
	11/8	-	Received instructions regarding forth coming offensive. Companies will be disposed of as follows. This state that Field Companies from each of 122nd and 150th Field Companies RE attached to 108th and 109th Brigade respectively for consolidation of strong points. 2 Sections from each of 122nd and 150th "Coys and sections of 121st coy for consolidating final objective to hold the outposts line. New 108th Brigade and arranged with them that 2 Sections of the Company attached to them would cross in old British front line at zero hour and should not be moved forward until situation warrants their use.	Q.

(A7092). Wt. W12839/M1293. 757,080. 1/17. D. D. & L., Ltd. Forms/C.2118/14.

WAR DIARY or INTELLIGENCE SUMMARY.

Summary of Events and Information

Place	Date	Hour	Summary of Events and Information	Remarks &c.
YPRES.	27/7	—	Officers and servant from Field Company 61st Division attached to us at forward billets to view area and job as the Division will be taking over from us after the offensive. Sergt Edwards wounded today.	B
	13/7	—	Track M.H. practically complete.	
	14/7	—	Track M.H. completed up to BLACK LINE with slight alterations. Dumps of material also complete. Bridging on forward portion of this track had a very bad time this evening as enemy put down intense barrage fire on two occasions and men had to be withdrawn until their barrages ceased. Sappers R. STEENBECK and T. R. STEENBECK killed.	B
	14/7	—	Received orders that evening of the R. STEENBECK had to be reconnoitred and if necessary or the bridges provided for various to cross by during attack. Infantry also has been told the near by and give us details information about these crossings. Lieuts T.H. KNOX and W. CROMWELL of this company had accordingly to go out with a party with portable bridges to reconnoitre, and, if necessary, put new bridges across. They found several crossings and one put is a new bridge. They were heavily shelled and both these officers were wounded, one man of party was killed and two others wounded. It seems very curious that with a well known obstacle such as R. STEENBECK running behind our line, which all experts must expect, that this line never been reconnoitred by infantry holding line in front of it, and	B

WAR DIARY OR INTELLIGENCE SUMMARY.

Summary of work and information:

Place	Date	Hour	
YPRES	14/7 (cont)	—	that it would therefore be necessary to send up RE Officers at the last moment to reconnoitre this.
	15/7 & 16/7	—	This Y day and attack to take place at 4.45 AM tomorrow morning. 16/7. Day of attack. Dispositions of 129th Field Company RE as follows at Zero hour 4.45AM.

1st Forward bullets. I 9 A 1.8. Lieut YOUNG MC.RE. attached to infantry. These were for serving final objective, is the consolidation behind the outpost line, and known as DOTTED RED LINE, and running (in 108A, or right brigade area) from D14A 25.80 – D14A 00.40, DWD 25.35. When consolidated there being used, others were to be sent to O.C. company (O.C. company being forward at Brigade Hq) from CRE and O.C. would then move then forward with materials to report at Brig. Hq on their way up. To this end immediate instructions materials for the party had previously been dumped in original German Front line, consisting of wire trench frames for infantry – 1 coil of barbed wire 6 medium screw pickets, and for the RE, 2 shovels or 2 picks is assisted to erect entries and spraw.

2. Old British front line. C29A 30.10. 2 sections officers Lieut. BENSON and Lieut. FAGAN (containing infantry company on 128.19). 2 RE sections and their attached infantry. These moved up from before zero, Lieut. Benson reporting to O.C. company forward bullets and took up their position half an hour before the zero. Lieut. Benson reporting to O.C. company at Brig. Hqrs when the party was in position.

These two sections were to assist in consolidation of starting points, previously chosen at GREEN HOUSE D13 85.50,

WAR DIARY or INTELLIGENCE SUMMARY

Summary of Events and Information

Place	Date	Hour		Remarks
YPRES	16/7 (cont)		TORONTO D.14.A.70.40 - HARTHA HOUSE D.14.C.3.6 - GALLIPOLI COPSE D.14.C.4.2. It was arranged with Brigade H.Q. that two sections should remain forward, and OC Company would be to see that work with the being moved forward, and OC Company would be to see that the work with the Rumour RE of that section. (Material in new dumps was dumped near to section).	
			At PACK CAMP. H.12.B.70.7.C 1. Whether infantry officer I would endeavour from 12th coy. 7 runners and observers from 16 MP.I.R (R). These were to move forward slowly to the dumps and that just back of our original front line and others were to report to OC Company at dugouts. The material to come trailing was to be taken up by these and so far forward as possible, and a dump formed near this over tract, and officer. It was to endeavour to carry dumps and this over tract and report positions of our own and enemy dumps to HQ. The selection of over-dictating field effective been fired this material.	(P)
			At House Ewin. H.2.C.0.8. 2nd in com and company - reverted temporarily to company - over (same times at Pack Camp) 20% casualties expect from before.	
			At Brigade Headquarters, WIEKTJE, C.28.B.40.66 O.C Company will orderly and runners.	(P)
			The situations were become definite enough to warrant the employment of the RE and the Pack Huts column was kept standing by behind over original front line and eventually sent back to Pack Camp. The two Brigade sections were kept in our original front line and were sent back to dumps that evening. The two sections in forward billets were never moved.	

WAR DIARY or INTELLIGENCE SUMMARY.

Summary of Events and Information

Place	Date	Hour		Remarks

YPRES | 16/7 (con) | | An unsuccessful attack of this description emphasizes the necessity of careful supervision of this work by Brigade R.E., by keeping Brigade and OC Company in touch with Brigade; these reports were not received by OC Pendus, so the situation when conveyed. The employment of RE. Before the operation it was suggested that it would be good to have the Brigade RE sections so far forward as possible at Zero hour, so that they could be moved forward quickly to follow the taking of an objective, to consolidate strong points against this there is the fact that of moves forward, they get beyond the control of Brigade and OC Company, as communication usually become bad, and they must time for receive their instructions from a Battalion commander who is totally about the situation in the immediate vicinity, and who may only know the RE sections forward too late, and in consequence move RE sections forward too late, and to involve them in a counter attack or send them to consolidate a position that is not definitely taken. | | |
| | 17/7 | | This happened in this attack, to the 2 Brigade. Received orders from CRE to send 2 sections up the evening to improve consolidation of YPRES LINE. Law 107th Brigade who stated that Brigade of Gordons was relieving them tonight, but that two Bn. Gordons were Butt Hop at 16.20 p.m. At Butt Hop were Batt Commanders of both Gordons, who stated that Butt Commanders answered no | Officer attention |

6

War Diary or Intelligence Summary

Summary of Events and Information

Place	Date	Hour		Remarks
YPRES	17/8/17 (cont)	—	To the Company commander in the Field that two latter Ushrs two to two only was got in but was not taking Black line, but was holding line toto in front of this, and was working forward tonight. Left Ghu this stores and returned to billets.	
WINNEZEELE	18/8	—	Marched over to full Company. 61st Divn ests. Certain marches took to VLAMERTINGHE and got stories to WINNEZEELE. Transport proceeded by march route.	
do.	19/8/17 to 22nd	—	At Winnezeele. Over hauling Company gear etc.	
On road	23rd	—	Marched to CASSEL, where we entrained and arrived at MIRAUMONT at about midnight. This were to trench proceeded by lorry to billets on main road S of LE TRANSLOY. Remainder trench by march route.	
LE TRANSLOY	25th	—	Went up to see line. The one taking over line from 9th Divisn	
"	26th	—	Two new officers reported. 2/Lieut G.E. EWENS and 2/Lieut A.J.B. ATKINSON.	
"	27th	—	They took over line with OC Tees Company 9th Divisn.	
"	28 6.29	—	Taking traders out of old German dugouts in vicinity	
ROYAULCOURT	30th	—	Company moved up to ROYAULCOURT, when Lieugneton, Lieut Ewis and a tutting detachment stopped	
			4 sectors moved up into forward billets in HAVRINCOURT wood.	
do.	31	—	Started work in two and in tutting areas.	

[signature]
Myndl
O.C. 122nd Field Coy R.E.

SECRET

O.C. 121 FdCoRE
O.C. 122 FdCoRE

G.O.C. is very anxious to do as much as is possible to hand over the BLACK LINE in a decent condition to the relieving Division

With this end in view each company will send up two sections tonight to assist 107 I.B. dividing the work by mutual arrangement between companies.

The work to be concentrated on is clearance of dugout entrances, drainage, and generally clearing out blown in portions so that troops can circulate from flank to flank.

Officers Commanding should send on an officer in advance to see the brigade and find out how they can keep adrift. (Brigade at MILL COT DUGOUTS).

The fact that 121 has been working by day, must not interfere with work tonight.

O.C. 121 Field Coy to see take action & pass to O.C. 122 Fd Co.

A Campbell
S/Colo
CRE 36 Div

17.8.17.
OC 121 AC
Noted & passed

AMewin Maj RE

17/8/17

Army Form C. 2118.

WAR DIARY
or
INTELLIGENCE SUMMARY.
(Erase heading not required.)

WO 24

Confidential

War Diary

of

122nd Field Coy. R.E.

36 Division

From

1st September 1917 to 30 Sept 1917

Volume 24.

[signature]
for OC 122 Field Coy R.E.

Army Form C. 2118.

WAR DIARY
or
INTELLIGENCE SUMMARY.
(Erase heading not required.)

Instructions regarding War Diaries and Intelligence Summaries are contained in F. S. Regs., Part II. and the Staff Manual respectively. Title pages will be prepared in manuscript.

Place	Date	Hour	Summary of Events and Information	Remarks and references to Appendices
RUYAULCOURT	1/2/17		Work in front line in progress, consisting of dug outs in front line. One dug out to accommodate two officers and one Shelter to accommodate widening, deepening, revetting and Vinetopping fire bays in localities between Support localities widening & deepening front line Communication trenches & general front line work.	
			Laying Canal du Nord at J.36.c.6.1. Repairing foundation for 60 cm track from Q.8a. 2.5. to K.32.c.6.4.	
	28/2/17		Pump house excavated and timbered to Coys water supply at Q.7d. central	

WAR DIARY or INTELLIGENCE SUMMARY

Army Form C. 2118.

Place	Date	Hour	Summary of Events and Information	Remarks and references to Appendices
RUMILCOURT	28/7		Distribution of Lectures altered. 3 Lectures at Vimy and week. Two sections doing front line work over. One Section doing all work in Bde. area outside front line. One Section at Headquarters, hutting detachment hutting up + Station at Headquarters took on Run work. Consisting in erection of Nissen Huts, Battalion H/qrs. G.Hqrs. Cook Houses, etc etc. & Erection of a tee [?] tramway.	
	29/6		Absent Sketches. 50 of to 100 attached infantry with drawn to unite for training.	
	26/8.		Major Hardie went to New H/qrs as acting C.R.E.	

M.A.Wright R.E.
for

Vol 25

Confidential

War Diary
- of -
122nd Field Coy. R.E.
- 36 Division -

From
1st October 1917 to 31st October 1917.

Volume 25.

WAR DIARY
or
INTELLIGENCE SUMMARY.
(Erase heading not required.)

Army Form C. 2118.

Place	Date	Hour	Summary of Events and Information	Remarks and references to Appendices
ROYAULCOURT.	1/7.	—	Headquarters, Nos. Two and One Sections at ROYAULCOURT. 3 Sections in HAVRINCOURT WOOD (LT CENTRE). 3 Forward Sections working as usual:— 2 Sections 1/6 and 3rd Battalion area: deep dugouts in Beaulieu in Front Line, continuing dugouts and working front line, reclm. of Coy. Hqrs. Captain Shelters. Cook houses and other work in and about Front line. 1 Section work in Brigade area behind Front line. Rear Section — Hutting and providing accommodation in billeting villages.	
	15/7/17	—	Changeover of 2 R.E. Sections. One of Forward Sections coming back to Royaulcourt and Rear Section relieving them at Forward billets. Work generally hampered by small supply of timber available for the purpose. Light revetting & cement especially being short. Weather bad, but trenches on the whole draining well.	
	31/7	—	Work continuing in line and in back areas.	

O.C. 122nd. FIELD COY. R.E.

Army Form C. 2118.

WAR DIARY
or
INTELLIGENCE SUMMARY.
(Erase heading not required.)

Vol 26

Confidential.

War Diary
of
122nd Field Coy. R.E.
36th Division
From
1st Nov. 1917 — to 30th Nov. 1917.

Volume 26

WAR DIARY
or
INTELLIGENCE SUMMARY.

Army Form C. 2118.

Place	Date	Hour	Summary of Events and Information	Remarks and references to Appendices
RUYAULCOURT	1/11/17		Headquarters Horse lines & 1 section at RUYAULCOURT. 3 sections in HAVRINCOURT WOOD. J 7 c central. 3 forward sections working as under:- Dugouts for T.M.B. - M.G. and dugouts in locations in front line. Shelter of elephant shelters & cookhouse for B" HQ." Water supply near Reserve Line. Artillery O.P. completed. Deepening widening and revetting front line. Back section working as under:- Accomodation at RUYAULCOURT & NEUVILLE.	
	10/11/17		1 forward section moved back to RUYAULCOURT. Work carried on as above.	
	16/11/17		2 Sections and 100 attached Infantry moved from forward area to rejoin the Company at RUYAULCOURT.	
I 29 d q.2.	16/11/17		Company & 100 attached Infantry moved from RUYAULCOURT to I 29 d q.2. I 25 d q.m. Work on accomodation for company, overhauling Weldon trestles & preparation of heavy bridging material. Attached Infantry working forward.	
	19/11/17		9 Panton & 9 F.S. wagon loaded with bridging material & parked at HERMIES.	

Army Form C. 2118.

WAR DIARY
or
INTELLIGENCE SUMMARY.
(Erase heading not required.)

Instructions regarding War Diaries and Intelligence Summaries are contained in F. S. Regs., Part II. and the Staff Manual respectively. Title pages will be prepared in manuscript.

Place	Date	Hour	Summary of Events and Information	Remarks and references to Appendices
I 29 d 9.2.	20/11/17 (Z" day)	8.30 a.	4 Sections with 100 attached infantry and teams for 18 wagons moved to HERMIES to await orders to commence work. Quarters in Catacombs.	
HERMIES J 29 g 5.7.	21/11/17	12.15 pm	2 Sections & 25 Inf. worked on a causeway crossing of CANAL DU NORD at K15 a 4.5. & on mule and infantry track from causeway to road at K 15 b 6.2. 2 Sections & 35 Inf. erected a wooden trestle bridge with ramps over canal du Nord at K 20 d 2.7. and on a mule & infantry track from bridge to road at K.15 d.A.1.	
	22/11/17		4 Sections & 100 infantry worked on corduroy track and causeway from K 13 d 7.3 to K.15 a 4.5.	
	23/11/17		4 Sections & 100 infantry stopped work on corduroy track and started work on overland routes from K.13 d 9.5. to K.15 a. 2.5.	
	26/11/17		1 Section worked on maintenance of overland route. 3 Sections and 100 attached infantry recommenced work on corduroy track about K 14 b 3.7. 2 Sections and 50 infantry moved into quarters in Lock 7 at K 9 c 1.8	
	27/11/17		3 sections and infantry worked as above. 1 section worked on erection of billets in HERMIES.	
	28/11/17		2 sections and infantry worked as above. 2 sections on billets in HERMIES.	
	29/11/17		2 sections moved from LOCK 7 to new billets in HERMIES. 2 sections worked on these billets.	
HERMIES J 30 a 6.4.	30/11/17		2 sections worked on siding from K.16 b 7.5 to K.17 c. 3.9. 2 sections carried rly. material from K.15 b 5.2. up to which point it was brought on light railway.	

Army Form C. 2118.

WAR DIARY
or
INTELLIGENCE SUMMARY.
(Erase heading not required.)

Vol 27

—CONFIDENTIAL—

WAR DIARY

OF

122ND FIELD COMPANY R.E

36 DIVISION

FROM

1st DECEMBER 1917 TO 31st DECEMBER 1917

Volume 27

Sheet 1
Army Form C. 2118.

WAR DIARY or INTELLIGENCE SUMMARY.

(Erase heading not required.)

Instructions regarding War Diaries and Intelligence Summaries are contained in F.S. Regs., Part II. and the Staff Manual respectively. Title pages will be prepared in manuscript.

Place	Date	Hour	Summary of Events and Information	Remarks and references to Appendices
HERMIES	1/2/17		Coy. employed wiring line from K.16.c.7.5 to K.17.c.3.9	
	2/2/17		Coy. employed making billets in HERMIES at J.30.a.6.4	
	3rd		Coy. moved from HERMIES to DESART WOOD & camped in open owing to non arrival of lorries with Kents. Horse lines	
	4th		moved from VELU to SORREL-LE-GRAND	
DESART WOOD	5th		Coy. employed wiring material Kenus by transport from METZ to RIBECOURT-TRESCAULT. Atkinson & Kell-Burn wounded by shell fire in RIBECOURT. Holy Coy. plus attacked inf. turned back at night to carry wire from RIBECOURT to Hindenburgh Support Line. Remainder of Coy. employed during day putting up Kents etc	
	6th		Coy. moved from DESART WOOD to HAVRINCOURT WOOD at Q.15.B. Horse lines remaining at SORREL-LE-GRAND. Coy. moved Kents & pitched tem in HAVRINCOURT WOOD as above. New routtant marched out behind front line	
HAVRINCOURT WOOD Q.15.B	7th		All Coy. employed wiring front line. Left HAVRINCOURT WOOD at 6.30 P.M. & arrived on job at 10 P.M. All material red to be carried up from Hindenburgh Support line to front line.	
	8th		No 2 & 3 Sections moved forward to dig out in Hindenburgh Support line at L.32.C.7.4. Attacked by enemy infantry. Returned to Brigade Camp. Shelled heavily in wood. Sgt. McKenna fatally wounded.	

Sheet 2
Army Form C. 2118.

WAR DIARY
or
INTELLIGENCE SUMMARY.

(Erase heading not required.)

Place	Date	Hour	Summary of Events and Information	Remarks and references to Appendices
METZ	10/2		No 1 & 4 Sections & HQ moved to billets in METZ at 9.20 O.C. 9. No 2 & 3 employed wiring front line.	
	11/2		New support line marked out for Pioneers to dig. This ran from L33b 30.35 to R 3 6 70.15	
	11/2 15/2 & 21		No 2 & 3 Sections employed on front line work. No 1 & 4 " " on billets in METZ marking out tracks to front line repairing trench bridges across roads. Transport employed drawing trench stores by night to Brigade forward dump.	
	16/2		No 2 & 9 Sections moved back to billets in METZ having been relieved by one section of 249 Field Coy. R.E.	
	17/2		Four Sections & H.Q. moved from METZ to camp in ETRICOURT. More lines would from SORREL LE GRAND to ETRICOURT.	
ETRICOURT	18/2		Dismounted portion of Coy. plus 3 G.S. Limbers & Supply wagon entrained at ETRICOURT for MONDICOURT Pas. Detrained at MONDICOURT PAS & proceeded to billets in GRINCOURT. Bony had accommodation wounded portion of Coy. less wagons on train moved by road for GRINCOURT stopping on the night of the 18/2 at COURCELLE. Remounted portion obtained from Division to move into billets at PAS. Dismounted portion of Coy. moved	
GRINCOURT	19/2			

Sheet 3
Army Form C. 2118.

WAR DIARY
or
INTELLIGENCE SUMMARY.
(Erase heading not required.)

Place	Date	Hour	Summary of Events and Information	Remarks and references to Appendices
GRINCOURT	19th		from GRINCOURT to PAS. owing to heavy snowfall mounted portion of Coy had to stay the night of 19th in BIENVILLERS.	
PAS	20th		Mounted portion of Coy arrived at PAS. Coy. employed making lines & wagon lines.	
	21st to 27th		Coy. refitted as far as possible but owing to bad state of roads great difficulty was experienced in getting stores. Certain tool carts overhauled also pontoon wagons & equipment. Coy. were inspected & clothing renewed.	
	27th		Mounted portion of Coy proceeded by march for BOVES, stopping the night of the 27th at PUCHVILLERS.	
	26th 9pm		Dismounted portion of Coy entrained at MONDICOURT PAS for BOVES. On arrival at BOVES the Coy. marched to billets in HAILLES. owing to bad state of roads Mounted portion of Coy. had to stay the night of the 26th at 24HOURS	
HAILLES	29th		Coy employed improving billets making sanitary arrangement. Mounted portion of Coy arrived at HAILLES.	

Sheet 4
Army Form C. 2118.

WAR DIARY
or
INTELLIGENCE SUMMARY.
(Erase heading not required.)

Place	Date	Hour	Summary of Events and Information	Remarks and references to Appendices
HAILLES	30th		Road between THEZY and HAILLES cleared of snow by Coy.	
	31st		Coy employed clearing roads so as to get transport through	

Army Form C. 2118.

WAR DIARY
or
INTELLIGENCE SUMMARY.

(Erase heading not required.)

Vol 28

122nd COY. ROYAL ENGINEERS
ULSTER DIVISION
No 2/26
Date 3/1/18

Confidential

War Diary
of
122nd Field Coy R.E.
36th Div.
from
1st January 1918
to
31st January 1918

Volume 28

T.N. Whinfield R.E.
for OC 122 Field Coy
R.E.

Army Form C. 2118.

WAR DIARY
or
INTELLIGENCE SUMMARY.
(Erase heading not required.)

Place	Date	Hour	Summary of Events and Information	Remarks and references to Appendices
HAILLES	1st 2nd 3rd		Dismounted portion of company were employed in physical exercises squad & company drill, and route marches, and in repairing rockwelling & dreg wagons & GS carts. Mounted section in clearing up harness etc.	
	4th		Inspected TSD carts and transport were inspected by a French General of Engineers.	
	5.		Pontoon bridge across Tuise river was thrown the rest of day spent in harness.	
	6.		Church parade at THEZY.	
	7.		Mounted and dismounted sections moved by road to BAYONVILLERS.	
BAYONVILLERS	8th 9th 10th		Company was refitted with clothes when necessary and rest of time spent in drilling and general training	
CARREPUIS	11th		Company moved by road to CARREPUIS. Left and kit were inspected	
	12			
DURY.	13		Company moved by road to DURY.	

Army Form C. 2118.

WAR DIARY
or
INTELLIGENCE SUMMARY.
(Erase heading not required.)

Instructions regarding War Diaries and Intelligence Summaries are contained in F. S. Regs., Part II and the Staff Manual respectively. Title pages will be prepared in manuscript.

Place	Date	Hour	Summary of Events and Information	Remarks and references to Appendices
DURY.	14		Company employed in fixing up billets in morning and bathed in afternoon	
	15/16		Part of Company employed in making notes boards and notice boards for Divn Canteen and Billets	
			Company marched to O.P. at ST CHRISTOPHE in morning, afternoon spent in making notice boards + fixing up billets	
BRAY ST CHRISTOPHE	17.		Repairs to billets and making notice boards. Section 3 + 4 dismounted section started in afternoon No 1 section under Lieut Ingram proceeded to ASSEVILLERS to work under R.A. for making deep abri at mayors Entry garden	
	18		No 2 section proceeded to OLLEZY to build Div H.Q.	
	19.			
	20		General work on billets in BRAY. + making notice boards. (H.Q. 39 + Le Trésor) No 1 + 2 in Sections dug arbi and Div HQ respectively	

2353 W↑ W2544/1454 700,000 5/15 D.D. & L. A.D.S.S./Forms/C. 2118.

WAR DIARY
or
INTELLIGENCE SUMMARY.
(Erase heading not required.)

Army Form C. 2118.

Place	Date	Hour	Summary of Events and Information	Remarks and references to Appendices
BR97 ST CHRISTOPHE	21		Patrol pumps at ROUPY and HAPPENCOURT taken over from French. No 1 Section on dug dugouts for RA. No 2 "employed on Div HQ. Reynolds on opening Billets making latrines etc in BR97.	
	22nd 23		No 1 Section employed on dugs dugouts for RA " 2 " " employed on Div HQ. C°3+4 Sections employed on making officers accommodation in OUGY and opening roads etc.	
	24 25		No 1 Section employed on dugs dugouts for RA No 2 " " employed on Div HQ.	
			No 3+4 employed in making alterations to H.Qrs at Gd SERACOURT and ARTEMPS etc in making motor tracks for ACM & to etc for bulls at night.	

Vol 29

Confidential

War Diary of
122nd Field Coy-
Royal Engineers
36th Div
Volume 29

From 1/2/18 to 28 2/18

WAR DIARY or INTELLIGENCE SUMMARY

Army Form C. 2118.

Place	Date	Hour	Summary of Events and Information	Remarks and references to Appendices
OPPY & FAMPOUX	1.2.18		No 1 Section went Tarjour employed in putting in dug outs for the main battery position at OLLEZY. Field Troop division No 2 section also on attachment in making extension to Reed at HQ. Remainder of Section employed in digging accommodation at Reed at ARRAS and HQs. OPPY ST RUPERT and HORSE SHOE at OPPY. 37 CHARTRUSE	
	2.2.18		Lt Munro returned from leave. Work carried on as before. Huts at FURNIERES and 2 finished at OPPY. Huts No 101 Section on dug outs for RA position on OPPY MUPPELZY	
	3.2.18 4.2.18		No 1 Section employed on dug outs for RA, No 2 Section on divisional HQ at OLLEZY, work started on Lewis Trench Mort. And on pipe line for tanks trough at AUBIGNY.	
	5.2.18		No 1 Section employed on dug outs for RA. No 2 Section on Div H.Q work being continued on huts at FLUVIERES, & erection of two Nissen huts started at same place.	
	6.2.18		Lt Chadworth joined the coy, work on Nissen huts completed and work on Lewis Trench Adrian huts at St Simon continued, other work as on 5.2.18. Baths at GD SERAUCOURT initiated	

Army Form C. 2118.

WAR DIARY
or
INTELLIGENCE SUMMARY.
(Erase heading not required.)

Place	Date	Hour	Summary of Events and Information	Remarks and references to Appendices
Bray St Christophe	7/1/18		Work on horse troughs at Artemps started rest of Company as on 6/1/18	
	9/1/18		Sections 1 & 2 same as yesterday other work as usual work on trough in St Simon stopped. Sixty troughs being completed work on troughs in Tugny finished 79 troughs completed	
	10/1/18 – 12/1/18		Work as usual	
	13/1/18		Repairs to an Adrian Hut in TUGNY started. Other work as usual.	
	14/1/18		Horse troughs at AUBIGNY finished. Other work as usual.	
	15/1/18 – 18/1/18		Same as usual.	
	19/1/18		Responsibility for preparation for demolition of 25 bridges over the ST. QUENTIN canal & the River SOMME was assigned to this Company. A section was given the work and reconnaissances of 9 bridges were made. Reports & the demolition schemes for demolition of the 9 bridges were approved by C.R.E.	
	20/1/18		Three sections were employed as previously the fourth being employed in preparations	

2333 Wt. W2544/1454 700,000 5/15 D.D.&L. A.D.S.S./Forms/C. 2118.

Army Form C. 2118.

WAR DIARY
or
INTELLIGENCE SUMMARY.
(Erase heading not required.)

Place	Date	Hour	Summary of Events and Information	Remarks and references to Appendices
	21/7/8		for demolition of 3 bridges. These preparations consisted of making & fixing boxes to take about 8 slabs of G.C. The outside box was fixed in the angle of the boom of a lattice girder & another box was made to fit inside it closely. This latter box contained the charge. Similar boxes were made for the bottom boom & the crossing of the diagonals. At the same time small dugouts were excavated in which to keep the charges till required & a position in a trench was chosen from which to fire the charge – 100% on calculated charges was allowed and 15 detonators No 13 MK III. for an exploder firing Trough 7.5" when packed firing Trough 7.5" when packed at 9.9 C 14 – less the company moved to billets vacated by 150th Field Coy. the section working on Div. H.Q. which remained at OLLEZY & the section attached to the R.A. which remained at A 30 b 08. 1 Section went straight up to forward billets also taken over from 150th Field Coy. at 6.6 a 7.7. They took over work on dugouts as below without cessation of progress. Dugouts are as follows:– 1. For Machine Gunners – at B 14 & 3 6. 2. " " " at B 21 C 9. 2. 3. " Infantry garrison at B 9 d 99.32. The fourth section worked ½ day on the back area Q' work & moved to at 9 c 14 = 7.77	

Army Form C. 2118.

WAR DIARY
or
INTELLIGENCE SUMMARY.
(Erase heading not required.)

Place	Date	Hour	Summary of Events and Information	Remarks and references to Appendices
GRAND SERAUCOURT S 10 77 G 9 c 1.4.	22/2/18		Forward section carried on work as yesterday. Section at headquarters worked on miscellaneous jobs such as screening roads, mortuary & canteen in GRAND SERAUCOURT, alterations to company billets, making mining frames and frames for S.A.A. & bomb recesses in the company workshops in the afternoon.	
	26/2/18		Section under R.A. was relieved by the section at Headquarters without work on R.A. dugouts being stopped.	
	27/2/18		Work as usual.	
	28/2/18		At present the Div. is organised in depth – 3 Bdes. in line of which 1 Bn. occupies the forward zone – 1 the Battle zone & the third is the Divisional Reserve. The field companies however do not conform to this – The 122nd Coy. is responsible for divisional work in the whole of the divisional front system –	

36th Divisional Engineers

122nd FIELD COMPANY R. E.

MARCH 1918

Army Form C. 2118.

WAR DIARY
or
INTELLIGENCE SUMMARY.

(Erase heading not required.)

Confidential

War Diary of
122nd Q.d Coy R.E.
March 1918.

WAR DIARY
or
INTELLIGENCE SUMMARY

Army Form C. 2118.

Place	Date	Hour	Summary of Events and Information	Remarks and references to Appendices
GQC.14.	1 3/10		The company is employed as under – 1 Section attached to R.A. for work on mined dug outs. 1½ Sections in forward billets working on mined dugouts at B.14.c.3.6. B.21.c.9.2. A.12.d.6.9. B.14.a.5.0. B.19.d.9.3. Ref Sheet 66° N.W. ½ Section employed at D.H.Q. at O.4.c.5.2.4. 1 Section at G.9.c.14. on miscellaneous work in Boles area.	
	2 3/10		A bridge was put across the canal at L.33.d.2.9. Sheet 66°D ¼40,000 It was a 75' gap – 2 Trestles + 2 pontoons being made. It is intended for use if a position in taking up on the Battle line – & it will then relieve traffic over the bridges at L.34.c.3.8. Sheet 66°D ¼40,000 16 men were employed. Remainder of coy as yesterday. – 3 Men employed on bridge approaches, remainder carried on with work in hand.	
	3/10		Site of bridge not deemed satisfactory by "G" as 17 men were employed on dismantling and re-erecting it at L.33.a.3.4. This incurred the use of an extra pontoon which was borrowed from 121st Field Coy R.E.	
	4 3/10			
	5 3/10		Work carried on – An anti-tank gun mounting was tested and proved satisfactory & 3 more mountings were practically completed in the Coy workshops.	
	20 3/10			

WAR DIARY
or
INTELLIGENCE SUMMARY.
(Erase heading not required.)

Army Form C. 2118.

Place	Date	Hour	Summary of Events and Information	Remarks and references to Appendices
G.G.14.	20/3/18	5.30p	Having received that an enemy attack was imminent. Orders temporary until stated that on the receipt of telegram "THUNDER" (code word for Hot Battle Stations) the Company was to return at once. All detachments reporting to company Headquarters at once at short notice.	
	21/3/18	4.30am	Very heavy bombardment commenced all along the line. Men were roused and ordered to stand by.	
		6.30am	"THUNDER" received. Company started to fall back to Dugouts. Breakfasts were cooked.	
		7am	Capt. Gibson reported from N.Y. Cottage at ESSIGNY STATION — he had tried to collect his section and had succeeded in getting most of them to the top of the bank at the cutting. He returned to get the rear man and had that the section in the thick fog. The enemy were being heavily gas shelled.	
		7am	Lt. EWENS R.E. reported that Tan he having done excellent work Withdrawn men from his dugouts to the cutting. He has been recommended to the Military Cross.	
		8.0a	Transport went to previously reconnoitred site at L.27.c.7.7. that 86 D Suppn at the exception of the tool carts which accompanied Lt. KNOX & Lt EWENS with me 1.2 & 3 Sechous to AVESNES. Here a footbridge was built across the canal L.33.c.47. Bridge completed at 9.0p. The material was cut on the site and was baulks were used spans about 75 ft. Roadway broken continuing. Two parts about 100 ft apart at MARSH FARM L.34.d.1.0 & that links and trestles and roadway for 23 ft long also two	

WAR DIARY or INTELLIGENCE SUMMARY

Army Form C. 2118.

Place	Date	Hour	Summary of Events and Information	Remarks and references to Appendices
	26/9		The C.O. rode up to near the bridge in course of construction returning to 2 S.G. 15. about 11.30 a.m. Lieut. FAGAN remained at headquarters until the remainder of No 2 & 4 sections arrived orders.	
		At 2.0 pm	orders received for No. 2 & 4 Secs to march to CRE of ALLERY 4th Infantry headquarters.	
		On arrival	Lieut. FAGAN was ordered to march to III company transport lines at L 5 & 35.6. C.O. was met at OCEZY.	
		On arrival of tpt at L 27 C 97. 3 Tpts wagons were sent to OCEZY for the purpose of drawing bridging material to L. Sub division of pontoon eqpt were in use - That however returned later in the day as they were not required. A shell destroyed the whole of the pontoon bridge at L33 a 3 at about 10.30 a.m. The houses were repaired within an hour. No details at yet known.	
		6.45	An accordance with orders to tpt. parked to tpt. L31 & 105 F tpt at L31 & 55. and bivouacked there. All officers were warned not the possibility of bicycles wire fed to the left behind on meeting enemy. No hygiene was available to remove them.
		70/45	Lieut. FAGAN joined tpt at 2 1/2 hrs.

WAR DIARY
or
INTELLIGENCE SUMMARY.
(Erase heading not required.)

Army Form C. 2118.

Place	Date	Hour	Summary of Events and Information	Remarks and references to Appendices
	21/3/18	10.0 p.	In accordance with orders received at 9.0p. the Div. R.E. H.Q. and details moved off to go to SOMMETTE EAUCOURT, the officer of No. 2 & 4 Sections starting off to the H.Q. After-orders were issued for the company to go to PITHON, these were received in time for the H.Q. motor lorry to go direct whereas lorries destined under Capt. WITHINGTON met to SOMMETTE EAUCOURT and got into billets before orders to go to PITHON were received. The C.O. met the party on SOMMETTE EAUCOURT.	
	22/3/18	3.30 am	That. Nos. 2 & 4 Sections were established at PITHON. No accommodation was available. Civilians were evacuating their homes about this time.	
		7.30 am	Lt KNOX & Lt EWENS joined Company & with Nos 1 & 3 Sections from MARSH FARM.	
		11.0 am	C.O. saw C.R.E. at ESTOUILLY. Supervised R.E. work & 2nd Lieut. Dunford at OLLEZY. was detailed from a party at ESTOUILLY. On to a bridge repair.	
		12.0 noon	Company moved to GOLANCOURT thro' HAM. arriving 2.15 p.m. Lt EWENS took two sections onward and cleared Stockade and loopholes from Coffin dump at HAM. Then he dumped at OLLEZY.	
	23/3/18	2.0 am	Wire received to work at S.O.P. to a new line being established back of canal between OLLEZY & HAM.	
		5.0 am	Company marched to stand by - by C.O. an orderlies came from HAM. stated that the enemy were in the town.	

(A7092). Wt. W12839/M1293. 75',000. 1/17. D.D. & L., Ltd. Forms/C.2118/14.

WAR DIARY
or
INTELLIGENCE SUMMARY.
(Erase heading not required.)

Army Form C. 2118.

Place	Date	Hour	Summary of Events and Information	Remarks and references to Appendices
	23/3/18	10.0a.m	Orders received to proceed to FLAVY-LE-MELDEUX on arrival to report about relief back to attend GOLANCOURT. Transport moved via V.18.b. V.12.b. V.18.d. MUIRANCOURT & CAMPAGNE and reported 12th at H.130. Tpt at U.23.a at 7.0 p.m. The sappers under C.O. & the 3 subs/Coys took up a position along the railway from F.M at BONNEUIL P.24.a to q.19.a 10.50 with H.Q.C. on their right along a line running to Q.26 central.	
	24/3/18		At midnight 23/24 enemy attacked and at 2.30a.m the company dropped back on to a line running from BONNEUIL CHATEAU to Q.26 central	
		7.0a.m	Company dropped back about 1000x to conform to movements on the flanks and took up a line with the French from P.34.d.3.3. to P.35.c.5.2. where they remained till 9.0 p.m.	
		9.0 p.m	The company was relieved and withdrew into support at a farm V.5.d.3.3. where the M.O. had formed an aid post. The C.S.M. & 2 spr. prepared bridge at CAMPAGNE for demolition & destroyed it successfully at 6.30 p.m. on 24th under orders from the French. It rejoined Coy at ARCHES at 7.0 a.m. on 25/3. The enemy went to within 1200 yards from the village which was destroyed –	
		12.15 a.m	Tpt. moved to MARGNY arriving 5.0 a.m. into a Nissen hut camp. (Margny T.9)	
	25/3/18	3.0 a.m	Company left farm at V.5 d.3.3. and marched to AVRICOURT halting for 3 hours at BEAULIEU U.19. Arrived AVRICOURT 2.0 p.m.	
		5.30 p.m	1 blanket per man and officers valises delivered to camp in AVRICOURT & preparations for staying the night commenced.	
		6.0 p.m	Orders received for company to march to ERCHES. Tpt. moved via ROYE, VILLERS les ROYE & ANDECHY arriving 9 p.m.	

(Apper). Wt. W12859/M1293. 73,080. 1/17. D.D. & L., Ltd. Forms/C.2118/14.

Army Form C. 2118.

WAR DIARY
or
INTELLIGENCE SUMMARY.
(Erase heading not required.)

Place	Date	Hour	Summary of Events and Information	Remarks and references to Appendices
	26th/3/18	2a.m.	Company arrived having had to make a large detour about making the detour round ROYE and therefore water was boiling and billets ready for the company when they arrived.	
		11.0 a.m.	Company ordered to take up a position N. of ERCHES in conjunction with 109 Bde. Tpt. left just as enemy commenced shelling village and moved with Bde. Tpt. to Le PLESSIER via GUERBIGNY DAVENESCOURT BOUSSICOURT BOUILLANCOURT MALPORT & GRIVESNES. arriving 5.30 p.m. At 7.30 p.m. enemy attacked the company and order to retire was carried out and a line was taken up behind ERCHES. Patrols gained contact with the enemy in ERCHES about 10.0 p.m. Major N.T.D. KERR was wounded here by a burst of M.G. fire. Lt. EWENS who was with him took him to a dressing station near 109 Bde. H.Q. Commencing to return he found that 109 Bde. HQ was surrounded and was ordered to return to Tpt. Lt. Tpt. having arrived at Le PLESSIER at 5.30 p.m. Capt. WITHINGTON received orders at 6.0 p.m. to prepare bridges between PIERREPONT & HARGICOURT for demolition. The A toolcarts had been left with the company at ERCHES so he arranged for a car from Division to get explosives from XVIII Corps who were at MOREUIL. The toolcarts however rejoined just as he was leaving so he took 2 A.A. cl[a]ss F.C. C.S.M. & 3 O.R. to the bridge at P.Y.C.O.2. arriving 10.0 p.m. Having found a boat, the night was spent preparing the bridge for demolition, 200 slabs being placed against the central pier which was of masonry.	

WAR DIARY or INTELLIGENCE SUMMARY.

Army Form C. 2118.

Place	Date	Hour	Summary of Events and Information	Remarks and references to Appendices
	29th		Other wooden footbridges were destroyed on 29th and a concrete footbridge alongside the main bridge was prepared with 24 slabs G.C. The bridge at O.12.d. 8.0. was a small stone brick arch the demolition of which would not cause sufficient delay to warrant its destruction. During 27th French troops came up and occupied the area, the C.O. being informed that the bridge was prepared for demolition. During the night of 27th/28th the enemy drew nearer and sappers were placed at scouts in PIERREPONT and Q.15.d. to give warning in case no warning was received from the French. About 8.0 a.m. a French engineer officer reported that he had been sent to see the preparations which had been made and that the French would take over during the day. On inquiry he was asked for more explosives and means of firing charges simultaneously as owing to the fact that no explosives were available and no instantaneous fuze is carried by a field company – safety fuze only was available. This arrived at 11.0 a.m. & a French corporal placed melinite petards on the iron girders and connected up the footbridge with detonating explosion. At 1.0 p.m. a French detachment of 9me Cie du Génie arrived with orders from Général LAVIGNY of 5me Div. Cavallerie to take over from EARP, WITTEN & TEW	

Army Form C. 2118.

WAR DIARY
or
INTELLIGENCE SUMMARY.
(Erase heading not required.)

Place	Date	Hour	Summary of Events and Information	Remarks and references to Appendices
			A letter since received from the French Sergeant states that the demolition of the bridges took place on the morning of the 29th and was entirely successful. Meanwhile the company under Lt. KNOX were holding the line ERCHES–Communication with 108th Bde. H.Q'rs. was cut & the company came under orders of 107th Bde. Owing to heavy pressure by the enemy the C.O. of 1st R.I.R. gave orders to retire on to a line	
27/3/18	6.0 a.m.		running from Q.8 central to Q.3 central. This was carried out about 6.0 a.m. 27/- The company in conjunction with the 9th R.I.F. & 12th R.I.R. were reformed here and made a small counter attack which succeeded in driving the enemy back on to the village of ERCHES. This enabled many wounded to be recovered and also some outposts who came	
	7.0 a.m.		in from the direction of GUERBIGNY. Owing to being again heavily shelled the company under orders from C.O. 9th R.I.F. fell back by stages to road running from HANGEST to DAVENESCOURT between Bouchoir & Piza. Here a line was formed and an outpost position under Lt. KNOX was taken up about 8.0 a.m. on the East side of the wood in Q.7. Shortly afterwards Lt. KNOX was wounded by shrapnel and was evacuated– 2nd Lt. FABAN who was in charge of the company's main line got into touch with the 30th Div. at R.32.b.	
	3.0 p.m.		Owing to heavy shelling from direction of WARSY Q.27 the company fell back on to a line running from J.30.c. to J.35.b. under orders of 107th Bde.	

Army Form C. 2118.

WAR DIARY
or
INTELLIGENCE SUMMARY.
(Erase heading not required.)

Instructions regarding War Diaries and Intelligence Summaries are contained in F. S. Regs., Part II. and the Staff Manual respectively. Title pages will be prepared in manuscript.

Place	Date	Hour	Summary of Events and Information	Remarks and references to Appendices
	27th	7.20 p.m.	The company was relieved and the Bde. returned to HANGEST. At midnight 27/28 the Bde. moved via PLESSIER-ROZAINVILLERS MOREUIL MAILLY THORY to SOURDON arriving 7.0 a.m.	
	28th		Here 11th FAGAN reported to C.R.E. with all sappers. At 3.0 p.m. he was ordered to rejoin Bde. at HANNEVILLE, where he arrived about 4.30 p.m.	
		6.30 p.m.	The tpt. under 11th EWEN'S R.E. meanwhile had left le PLESSIER & arrived at speed during the night at AUBVILLERS. It marched to SOURDON where 11th FAGAN joined it and then on to HANNEVILLE. Lt. BENSON took 2 Twette wgns, 2 tool carts & pack mules to ABBEVILLE on 27th.	
		10.0 p.m.	CAPT. WITHINGTON rejoined the company at HANNEVILLE. The tpt. two tons 2 limbers & 1 toolcart under 11th FAGAN joined the R.E. & Pioneer tpt. in the woods at G26	
	29th	7.30 p.m.	3 Companies under command of Major FORDHAM moved to VELENNES via BERNY TUNEL. ORESMAUX & WAILLY arriving at Staff 5.30 a.m. 30th.	
	30th		3 Companies tpt. under Maj. OTWAY moved also the company's tpt. under 11th FAGAN arriving at 9.0 a.m.	
	30th	5.30 p.m.	Company moved to SALEUX with orders to entrain at 11.0 p.m. Night was spent in the train on the road waiting for the train which finally arrived about 7.0 a.m. 31st.	
	31st		The company entrained & detrained at GAMACHES about 3.30 p.m. The tpt. which had moved by road arrived at 7.30 p.m. where the company spent a well earned night's rest. Good billets were found at DARGNIES.	

Army Form C. 2118.

WAR DIARY
or
INTELLIGENCE SUMMARY.
(Erase heading not required.)

Instructions regarding War Diaries and Intelligence Summaries are contained in F. S. Regs., Part II. and the Staff Manual respectively. Title pages will be prepared in manuscript.

Place	Date	Hour	Summary of Events and Information	Remarks and references to Appendices
			Summary of Casualties.	
			Major M.T.D. KERR. Wounded 26/3/18.	
			Lt. T.K. KNOX " 27/3/18.	
			Killed 5	
			Wounded 13	
			Wounded & missing 1	
			Missing 19	
			――	
			38	
			Total between 20th & 31st 2 Officers	
			38 O.R.	

36th Divisional Engineers

122nd FIELD COMPANY R. E. ::: APRIL 1918.

WAR DIARY
or
INTELLIGENCE SUMMARY.

(Erase heading not required.)

Army Form C. 2118.

122 Fd Coy RE

War Diary
of
the
122nd Field Company
Royal Engineers 36th Div
for
April 1st to 30th
1918

Volume 31

Army Form C. 2118.

WAR DIARY
or
INTELLIGENCE SUMMARY.
(Erase heading not required.)

Instructions regarding War Diaries and Intelligence Summaries are contained in F. S. Regs., Part II. and the Staff Manual respectively. Title pages will be prepared in manuscript.

Place	Date	Hour	Summary of Events and Information	Remarks and references to Appendices
DARGNIES near FAMACHES	1/9/18		Company employed in making wagon covers, repairing billets and refitting - Lt. BENON arrived with 2 G.S. wagons & 2 foot carts from ABBEVILLE.	
	2/9/18		Company employed as on 1st & the men were billeted in company lofts. Orders received to stand by to move on the 3rd.	
	3/9/18		Tpt. marched off at 11.15 p.m. to entrain at EU.	
	4/9/18		Dismounted branch marched off at 12.30 a.m. to entrain at EU. Entraining completed at 7.0 a.m. and the Company arrived at ROEXPOEDE at 4.0 p.m. 3 lorries conveyed the dismounted branch to HERZEELE.	
ROEXPOEDE near BERGUES HERZEELE	5/9/18		Tpt. arrived 4.0 a.m. Capt. WITHINGTON met C.R.E.s of 1st & 36th Divn at 2.0 p.m. at CANAL BANK CAMP C.25.d.2.2. Sheet 28 & arranged details of relief of 23rd Field Coy by 122nd Army Troops R.E.	
	6/9/18		2 lorries conveyed 50 O.R.s & 3 officers to ILMINSTER CAMP C.27.b.2.3. Sheet 28 arriving 5.30 p.m. Billeted in huts unoccupied by 23rd Field Coy.	
	7/9/18		No 1 Section carried on work at 8.0 a.m. at PHEASANT FARM O.P. No 2 Section remained in camp. 23rd Field Coy marched out at 11.0 a.m. Tpt. arrived at NURAT CAMP B.30.a at 4.0 p.m. Capt. W. SMYTH arrived & took over command of the Company	

WAR DIARY
or
INTELLIGENCE SUMMARY.
(Erase heading not required.)

Army Form C. 2118.

Place	Date	Hour	Summary of Events and Information	Remarks and references to Appendices
ILMINSTER CAMP NEAR WIELTJE	8/4/18		No:1 Section carried on w/R work at PHEASANT FARM O.P. Proposed work on Pill-Boxes on the ARMY BATTLE ZONE was recounted arranged with the C.R.E. ABZ + the C.E. of Corps. ii Lieut H. ROWAN HODGE joined the Company	
	9/4/18		No:1 Section commenced work on Reinforced Concret Pill-Boxes in the RESERVE SYSTEM of the ARMY BATTLE ZONE. Three new pill-boxes to be constructed + has German Pill-Boxes at FYSH FARM + CATWICK COT to the commenced. Remainder of Coy. stayed in Billet for fatigues etc.	
	10/4/18		Work carried on with the Pill-Boxes as before. ii Lt. EWERS proceeded to the Store Lines at MURAT CAMP. ii Lt. Chadworth arrived from the Store Lines. Reinforcements arrived 1 Sgt. + 52 other ranks. Lt. BENSON took over his duties as Stores Officer to the C.R.E.	
	11/4/18		Pill-Box work carried on as before. 5 man reinforcements arrived. Reinforcements work on hand, so has ALARM POST; in event of heavy bombardment. Reinforcements medically inspected.	

WAR DIARY
or
INTELLIGENCE SUMMARY.

(Erase heading not required.)

Army Form C. 2118.

Place	Date	Hour	Summary of Events and Information	Remarks and references to Appendices
ILMINSTER CAMP. NEAR WEILTZE	12/4/18		Pill Box work carried on as before. Reconnaissance of the Bridges on the Divisional front of the STEENBEEK for the purpose of preparation for demolition.	
	13/4/18		Nos. 1 & 2 Sections working on Pill Boxes. Party of No. 3 & 4 Section prepared 8 BRIDGES on the STEENBEEK for demolition. Lt. KNOX arrived from the Base. Whilst MERCIER carried from 150th Fd. Coy. R.E. 4 more reinforcements arrived.	
	14/4/18		No. 1 Section stood by. No. 2 & part 4 Section carried on with work on Pill Boxes. No. 3 & part 4 Section carried on with preparation of bridges.	
	15/4/18		Nos. 1 & 2 Section prepared training grounds M of ST JULIEN. No. 4 Section prepared the large Pill-Box at ST JULIEN for demolition. Nos. 1 & 3 Sects. All preparations were completed to-day. 1000 L ammunition Evening. The remainder of the company moved into huts on the CANAL BANK.	

Army Form C. 2118.

WAR DIARY
or
INTELLIGENCE SUMMARY.
(Erase heading not required.)

Place	Date	Hour	Summary of Events and Information	Remarks and references to Appendices
YSER CANAL BANK.	16/4/18		Demolitions completed by early morning. Whole Company moved to the CANAL BANK. Horse Lines left MURAT CAMP & proceeded to CARDOEN CAMP, near ELVERDINGHE. Nos: 1 + 2 Sections worked on wiring near WEILTJE, at night.	
	17/4/18		Early morning, No: 4 Section completed demolition near WEILTJE in 1st Bn 41st Div. front. Parades for Pt intputs etc. for remainder. Billets where obtained, for ½ Company, at CARIBOU CAMP, near the storm line.	
	18/4/18		No: 3 Section. Nos: 1 + 2 Sections moved to billets at CARIBOU CAMP	

Army Form C. 2118.

WAR DIARY
or
INTELLIGENCE SUMMARY.
(Erase heading not required.)

Instructions regarding War Diaries and Intelligence Summaries are contained in F. S. Regs., Part II. and the Staff Manual respectively. Title pages will be prepared in manuscript.

Place	Date	Hour	Summary of Events and Information	Remarks and references to Appendices
	19/4/18		Nos 1 & 2 Sections training & refitting – Nos 3 & 4 Sections worked with 2 Bn Inniskillings on preparation of accommodation & defences in reserve line in C.27 & C.28	sheet 28
	20/4/18		No.4. Section took over preparation for demolition of WIELTJE dugouts from 223rd Field Coy 41st Division & started improving them	
	21/4/18			
	22/4/18		work as above till 5.0p – at which time relief of Nos 3 & 4 Sections was effected by Nos 1 & 2 Sections	
	23/4/18		Work carried on & O.P. for Div Observation commenced at C.22.b.9.2. sheet 28. No.2 Section started mining WIELTJE dugouts so that the leads will be kept in the dugouts all the way & so will break out of back of fine. The dugout is about 200' long & has 19 entrances. Each entrance is charged with 15 slabs half way down packed against top sill. Safety fuze to Fuze Instanteous in leads of Ignition. Electrical circuit divided into two firing A & B circuits. No.1 Section working on Reserve Line C.7/C.4b.	
	25/4/18		Nos 3 & 4 training at CARIBOU CAMP	

Army Form C. 2118.

WAR DIARY
or
INTELLIGENCE SUMMARY.
(Erase heading not required.)

Place	Date	Hour	Summary of Events and Information	Remarks and references to Appendices
	26/4/18		Following way points were prepared by No 1 Section. Junction of BUFF, VIELTJE & TURCO roads - Cross roads of ADMIRALS & BUFF - HAMMONDS CORNER - Cross roads 200yds E of BURNT farm - RE at c.28.d.6.7. - Level crossing at IRISH FARM. Also following by No 2 Section. VIELTJE fork roads - Junction of ADMIRALS road in junction of OXFORD rd & VIELTJE roads 5' to 10' deep were loaded with 300 lb. to 500 lb. Ammonal & well tamped. Northwound to June of CALIBAN reserve communication	
	27/4/18	9 p.m.	During night of 26/27th the above company moved to CARIBOU camp less H.Q. demolition party of 1 NCO & 6 OR for VIELTJE Shopment + 1 NCO & 10 OR for No 1 Section as demolition party for the road under H.Q. Charterworks. 11th Regim. + OC stayed in the area. Test lout for signals detailed.	
	28/4/18		Rest of Coy & Burial lines moved to Camp 200 yards Nr of International Corner Sheet 28 A 3.C 14. Forward party supervised work in C.20a on a front	
	29/4/18		No 1 section went back to Canal Bank - Worked on deepening Hill top & Minoro fronts for demolitions - No 3 Section commenced work on yellow line between A.24.b.6.8. + A.30.b.6.0 - in conjunction with 103 Bdes.	

WAR DIARY
or
INTELLIGENCE SUMMARY.

(Erase heading not required.)

Army Form C. 2118.

Place	Date	Hour	Summary of Events and Information	Remarks and references to Appendices
	30/9		No 4 Section commenced with work on 9 metre line between B 20 a 87 & B 26 d 37 work as yesterday — Tactical situation during this week has changed daily, Almost owing to the menace in the Kemmel area, and that it has been difficult to arrange priority of work. All ammunition in batteries was necessarily spent out due largely to east in strong charges and to very close touch with Batts & Bns concerned	

Army Form C. 2118.

WAR DIARY
or
INTELLIGENCE SUMMARY.
(Erase heading not required.)

WC 32

WAR DIARY.

of the

122ND Field Company Royal Engineers. 36TH DN.

from

May 1st — May 31st
1918.

O.C. 122nd Fd Coy RE

*[Stamp: 122ND COY. ROYAL ENGINEERS * ULSTER DIVISION]*

CONFIDENTIAL

Army Form C. 2118.

WAR DIARY
or
INTELLIGENCE SUMMARY.
(Erase heading not required.)

Place	Date	Hour	Summary of Events and Information	Remarks and references to Appendices
	1/5/18		Company situated as follows — 1½ sections standing by for demolishing dugouts roads and full bores under C.O. at Canal Bank. No 3 & 4 section moved today to BORDER CAMP after work on "green and yellow line. ½ section also worked on green line that returned to horse lines on completion. Horse lines and office at RIPLEY CAMP near International corner sheet 28 A2L22.	
	3/5/18		Rear H.Q." moved to BORDER CAMP A30 b 35. C.O. returned to new Rear position. Capt. Whittington went forward. New position taken up from Bigge Tracks forward of Bridge junction to join up with the Belgians in front of ELVERDINGHE.	
	5/5/18		Work as usual. Forward section on work in the 107½ Bde. area.	
	7/5/18			
	8/5/18		No L. section relieved No1 Sec. & ½ No2 Sec. at Canal Bank after work — No incidents of note caused. Rdn. Battle H.Q. & Bn. Battle H.Q. for green line advanced.	
	9/5/18		Work as usual.	
	10/5/18		Rear section on green line including an R.A.P. at Hospital gate & preparations for destroying PELISSIER F". Bridge 4.2.45 to HILLTOP F"	
	11/5/18		Rear section and H.Q. moved from BORDER CAMP to HOSPITAL F.7. camp	

WAR DIARY or INTELLIGENCE SUMMARY

Army Form C. 2118.

Place	Date	Hour	Summary of Events and Information	Remarks and references to Appendices
	12/7/15		Work as before. Proceeded reconn. it consisted posts in outpost line. On 15th the Company took over the responsibility for screening & bridges	
	15/7/15		on the Canal from 150th Bde. R.E.	
	17/7/15		No 1 & 2 Coy moved to Canal Bank. Rear HQ & C to RIPLEY. No 4 Coy to RIPLEY	
	18/7/15		C.O. to Canal Bank. Capt to RIPLEY. No 1 Coy on Bde work. No 2 Coy in demolition East of Canal. No 3 Co. on demolition of Canal bridges. No 4 Coy Training	
	19/7/15		No 1 Pl. Coy on Infantry shacks and tram from N of Buffs Road, Wieltje E of Canal. Working parties clearing field of fire etc. No 2 Section in order. E & C bde. Left Y.p. Farm & WIELTJE Dugouts. New Charge Sh R.5 Uhr 2 [unclear] mines put in to find what to replace the V.C. dets. not 4 Kp dugout to hold 4 men. No: 4 deep, 15" pipes full of [unclear] [unclear] 8 [unclear] a Coy's work. Pilly a Co [unclear] [unclear] [unclear] unused, wheresoever ready [unclear] some a [unclear] one cd. Rthur and B Col [unclear] a bombers but the that ed. O Col. born late fuses in RE charge the work tempts, end of R.F. photographs firm trench ready to fire Wellington Canal No: 3 Sect. manned holes in the Canal	

WAR DIARY
or
INTELLIGENCE SUMMARY.

(Erase heading not required.)

Army Form C. 2118.

Instructions regarding War Diaries and Intelligence Summaries are contained in F.S. Regs., Part II. and the Staff Manual respectively. Title pages will be prepared in manuscript.

Place	Date	Hour	Summary of Events and Information	Remarks and references to Appendices
	20/5/18		War carried on as before. Night for Bde.	
	21/5/18		to Mousetrap Trench for the 91st R.I. Frontier	
			No. 4 Platoon relieved No. 1 Section who proceeded to rear billets for training	
	22/5/18		War carried on as before	
	23/5/18			
	24/5/18			
	25/5/18			
	26/5/18		No. 1 Section relieved No. 2 Section at the Canal Br. R. No. 2 Section proceeded to rear billets for training. No. 1 Section took over No. 3 Section from Q to demolition of Canal Bridge. No. 3 Section took over Bdge. wk. R. No. 4 Section. No. 2 Section took over S.H.T.P. + M.E.L.T.N.E. Dugouts & w.and over from No. 2 Sect. No. 4 Section took over Near + Blues + Captains Post command at Canal Br. R.	
	27/5/18		Major Renaud to Near + Blues + Captains Post command at Canal Br. R. Lieut. Rain Proceeded to Cap. Post. A2 (relief, or present) of heavy shelling at International Corner. (RIPLEY CAMP) Dr. HILLMAN slightly wounded + Thieved.	

WAR DIARY
or
INTELLIGENCE SUMMARY.

(Erase heading not required.)

Army Form C. 2118.

Instructions regarding War Diaries and Intelligence Summaries are contained in F. S. Regs., Part II. and the Staff Manual respectively. Title pages will be prepared in manuscript.

Place	Date	Hour	Summary of Events and Information	Remarks and references to Appendices
	28/8		WoR carried on as before. Casualty tables reported by H.Q. at A.D. Stns.	
	29/8/18		Bios R. handed over to R.Q. 121st Field Bigs. H.Q. + 3 Sechs Bivouac near BROMWELL CAMP near ELVERDINGHE. No 2 Sec in Tps + No 4 in R. the D. O.I.G Bys. at 163 + 173 Battling Zeloo. E.B. Canal Rafts. This Sec took over work for 121 Infan Brig on GREEN LINE	
	30/8/18		+ BRIELEN defences. No. 1 Sec on GREEN LINE No. 3 Sec on BRIELEN defences No. 4 Sec construct Battle - BOE HQ + Aid Posts - GREENLINE + BRIELEN DEFENCES.	
	31/8/18		Nos: 1, 3, 4 Sections + H.Q. proceeded to HOSPITAL FARM CAMP. Summary of Sickness Capn on Jepson BRADBURY alleged absent. Captain left for Home leave. Taken to Rowed to CALAIS + Returng Camp	

Army Form C. 2118.

WAR DIARY
or
INTELLIGENCE SUMMARY.
(Erase heading not required.)

Vol 33

Confidential

War Diary
of the
122nd Field Coy Royal Engineers
36th Div
from
1st June to 30th June
1918.

Vol 33

to OC 122 Field Coy RE

Army Form C. 2118.

WAR DIARY
or
INTELLIGENCE SUMMARY.

(Erase heading not required.)

Instructions regarding War Diaries and Intelligence
Summaries are contained in F. S. Regs., Part II.
and the Staff Manual respectively. Title pages
will be prepared in manuscript.

Place	Date	Hour	Summary of Events and Information	Remarks and references to Appendices
HOSPITAL FARM CAMP.	1/6/18		W.R. on BRIELEN & GREEN LINE continued.	
	2/6/18		Church Parade etc. No. 2 Section returned from the Canal Bank.	
	3/6/18		Handed over the BRIELEN & GREEN LINE W.R. to BELGIAN ENGINEERS; and marched to camp at L3.B.78. Improving camp site, & erecting screen huts at D.H.Q. - COUTHOVE CHATEAU.	
	4/6/18		Erecting huts at D.H.Q.	
BALL CAMP. (L3.B.78)	5/6/18 6/6/18 7/6/18		and TRAINING of men by sect. officer.	
	8/6/18		Party sent to take over W.R. on BLUE LINE. Church Parade. Inspection Parade 3 Coys. by C.R.E.	
	9/6/18 10/6/18		Coys. now W.R. on BLUE LINE but all 4 sections.	

Army Form C. 2118.

WAR DIARY
or
INTELLIGENCE SUMMARY.
(Erase heading not required.)

Instructions regarding War Diaries and Intelligence Summaries are contained in F. S. Regs., Part II. and the Staff Manual respectively. Title pages will be prepared in manuscript.

Place	Date	Hour	Summary of Events and Information	Remarks and references to Appendices
BALL CAMP.	11/6/18		Company prepared to PRICE CAMP PROVEN. (F.7.c.5.2). 2 n.c.os and 6 of A.T. Ra-ways for transport of Sections to the war and release lorries.	
PRICE CAMP PROVEN - [F.7.c.5.2]	12/6/18		All 4 Sections transferred to 2.45 a.m. Parade 3-30. a.m. to get to Train at PUGWASH for work in BLUE LINE. Dinner at	
	13/6/18			
	14/6/18		3-30 p.m. completed. 4 ohys work.	
	15/6/18		Trip to 6 men injured many colliding with a head of a Tank. three shot to hospital.	
	16/6/18		Burial Parade. Corps reported to wait.	
	17/6/18		War as before in BLUE LINE.	
	18/6/18		Double gave obtaining stores for Corps through Divn.	
	20/6/18		Works Cmdt. Greatly reduced transfer work to Div Orders. Yeomanry Major	
	21/6/18			
	22/6/18			

W.O.P. to 150 F. Coy. R.E.

Army Form C. 2118.

WAR DIARY
or
INTELLIGENCE SUMMARY.
(Erase heading not required.)

Instructions regarding War Diaries and Intelligence Summaries are contained in F. S. Regs., Part II. and the Staff Manual respectively. Title pages will be prepared in manuscript.

Place	Date	Hour	Summary of Events and Information	Remarks and references to Appendices
PRICE CAMP	23/6/18		Fatigues & training	
PROVEN.	24, 25/6/18		Training. Musketry.	
(F) 1.6.5.2	26/6/18		WnR a Horse Show at Proven Aerodrome	
	27/6/18			
	28/6/18		Coy. proceeded to RUBROUCK for Musketry. Entrained at PROVEN - mtd. parties by road.	
	29/6/18 30/6/18		Coy. fired Musketry Course on 100 yd. & 30 yd. Ranges at RUBROUCK	

Army Form C. 2118.

WAR DIARY
or
INTELLIGENCE SUMMARY.
(Erase heading not required.)

WO 34

War Diary
of the
122nd Field Coy Royal Engineers
38th Div
1st July to 31st July
1916

No 34

Wilkinson / Capt. R.E.
to OC 122 Field Coy R.E.

WAR DIARY
or
INTELLIGENCE SUMMARY.

Army Form C. 2118.

Place	Date	Hour	Summary of Events and Information	Remarks and references to Appendices
Roubrouck	1/7/18		Meeting Divers. Company late. 6 yeoman of 100 yds + 20 yds jumps.	
St Jans-tu	2/7/18		Company moved from ROUBROUCK to ST JANS-DE-BIZEN. (Bell camp)	
BIZEN				
	3/7/18		Company moved by route march from ST JANS-DE-BIZEN to EECKE	
EECKE	4/7/18		Company moved by route march to EECKE Sheet 27	
	5/7/18		Work on Reservoir R.26.b.5. on ... Road ... R.19. b. 4.2.2 and	
			Company ... at ...	
			Training	
	6/7/18		Advance party to R. our HQ at ... 7/62 P.M.	Monte. Dere
			Coys. Nos: 2. 3. 4. Returns left EECKE at 9 a.m ... to (S.27.) R19.4.87	
	7/7/18		Mont-de-CATS. ½ Col. H & R.E. GER Provided H.R.E.	
			From ... 105. 1 + 3 ... left EECKE at 8 p.m	
			Relieved ... R. 28. + 28. M36. C.H. + M35.d. Central respectively	
			Brigade at Dec. + 28. farm at ... (S.27.) Q32 6.56.1	
	8/7/18		Advance Series moved ... left EECKE at 9 a.m referred to (S.27). R19.4.87	
			H.Q - Nos: 2. 3. 4 Returns ...	
			Commenced work on Div. H.Q. water dugout, also completed 3 dugouts R19 a. 4.8	
			+ repairs to camouflage	
			Fit Char. B, Artz. WATER SUPPLY ...	

Army Form C. 2118.

WAR DIARY
or
INTELLIGENCE SUMMARY.

(Erase heading not required.)

Instructions regarding War Diaries and Intelligence Summaries are contained in F. S. Regs., Part II. and the Staff Manual respectively. Title pages will be prepared in manuscript.

Place	Date	Hour	Summary of Events and Information	Remarks and references to Appendices
MONT-DES-CATS	8/7/18		No. 1 & 3 Sections —	
			No. 1 L.G. moved up prior to Bde H.Q. (B.29.C.4.2.) having previously constructed frame work of entire Reserve Bn H.Q. dugout at (M.33.c.4.9.) (inches)	
			LEFT Bn.	
			No. 5 L.G. commenced work on ERMITAGE LINE (B—24—c.4.9)	
			having dug—to bivs—at M26.c.4.9	
	9/7/18		No. 2 L.G. moved forward to M.20.C.71	
	10/7/18		Work carried on as before	
	11/7/18			
	12/7/18		No. 7 Section commenced work on (Coys) BLUE LINE from Lt ERMITAGE to R.3.0.6. Left Div Boundary — M27.c.	
	13/7/18		No. 4 Section commenced second BERTHEN Road	
	14/7/18		Work as above	
	15/7/18			

WAR DIARY or INTELLIGENCE SUMMARY.

Army Form C. 2118.

Place	Date	Hour	Summary of Events and Information	Remarks and references to Appendices
MONT-DE-CATS	16/7/18		No. 1 Section Commenced Construction of Visual O.P. on MONT DE CATS and a B.C. Post at RETHEN for C. 153 R.F.A. O.P. Consists of reinforced concrete roof (approx 5ft) on lower slope of MONT-NOIR overlooking Center Line on BAILLEUL left.	
			METEREN. B.C. Post. Pit about 8' deep. Concrete Shelter under E. Reinforced concrete sand-bag cement shelter east + front of trench. ditto No 2 S.C. under BLUE LINE on right of No 3 Section.	
	17/7/18		Work as above	
	18 19 20/7/18 21 22			
	23/7/18		Company relieved by 199 Coy R.E. No 2 + 6 Sections handed to 6? DE MERSVERDE Down H.Q. marched other line at BRONA. (R.32.b.5.6)	

Army Form C. 2118.

WAR DIARY
or
INTELLIGENCE SUMMARY.
(Erase heading not required.)

Instructions regarding War Diaries and Intelligence Summaries are contained in F. S. Regs., Part II. and the Staff Manual respectively. Title pages will be prepared in manuscript.

Place	Date	Hour	Summary of Events and Information	Remarks and references to Appendices
LE LAURIER.	24/7/18		Work on Saw-mill. Nursing Notice Boards etc. 8mn working at D.H.Q. (TERDEGHEM) Lewis gun Training	
	25		As above.	
	26			
	27			
	28			
	29/7/18		2nd Lieut A.J. Houlden R.E. joined the Coy on transfer from F.62 — £64 D.E	
			under a tent.	
	30/7/18		Programme of work as above	
	31/7/18			

Army Form C. 2118.

Vol 35

WAR DIARY
or
INTELLIGENCE SUMMARY.
(Erase heading not required.)

Confidential

War Diary
of the
122nd Field Coy. Royal Engineers
36th Div
1st August to 31st August
1918

R J Lee Capt
for OC 122nd Field Coy R.E.

Vol 35

Army Form C. 2118.

WAR DIARY
or
INTELLIGENCE SUMMARY.
(Erase heading not required.)

Place	Date	Hour	Summary of Events and Information	Remarks and references to Appendices
EECKE	1/8/18		Nos 2 & 4 Section working at GODEWAERSVELDE dump. H.Q and remainder at EECKE	
	2nd		ditto. Then given instruction in Lewis gun.	
	3rd			
	4th 5th 6th		Parade for presentation of V.C. to Lieut KNOX.	
	7th		H.Q. + Nos 4 + 3 Section mov to Mont des CATS, Nos 2 & 4 Sect from GODE DUMP to MT NOIR	
	8th		Coy relieved by 150th Field Coy on right 7th/8th in the forward area	
MONT DES CATS	9th		Work commenced on BLUE LINE incl. construction of O.P's etc. Work greatly hindered by hostile fire. L/C R wounded & later died of wounds	
	10th		Work on BLUE LINE	
	11th 12th		ditto ditto	

Army Form C. 2118.

WAR DIARY
or
INTELLIGENCE SUMMARY.
(Erase heading not required.)

Place	Date	Hour	Summary of Events and Information	Remarks and references to Appendices
Mt des CATS	13/8/18		C.R.E. recct H.Q. of Coy. Work continues on BLUE LINE	
"	14th		Work on BLUE LINE. O.P's, C.T's etc.	
	15th		ditto Infantry track from BERTHEN to ST JANS CAPELLE, Rd.	
	16th		Work on BLUE LINE and accommodation for 2 battalions in the line	
	17th		ditto	
	18th		CAPT. WITHINGTON left Coy to report to COMMANDANT Instructors School BERKHAMPSTEAD	
	19th		No 3 Sec moved from Mt des CATS to Mt NOIR. Work as usual	
	20th		Work on BLUE LINE and accommodation for 2nd R.Ir. Fus.	
	21st		H.Q. & No 1 Sec move to Mt NOIR from Mt des CATS.	
Mt NOIR	22nd		Work same as above but with addition of dugouts in QUARRY at Mt NOIR	
	23rd		ditto	
	24th		ditto	
	25th		ditto	
	26th		CAPT. N.J. LEE R.E. arrived to assume duties of 2nd I/c	
	27th		Work the same	
	28th		ditto C.R.E. visits the H.Q. forward.	
	29th		Work the same. Most of the work being concentrated on getting the 4 inclines for Dugouts in QUARRY down to drift before relief.	

Army Form C. 2118.

WAR DIARY
or
INTELLIGENCE SUMMARY.
(Erase heading not required.)

Place	Date	Hour	Summary of Events and Information	Remarks and references to Appendices
MT NOIR	30/8/18		Coy relieved on work by 150th Field Coy. Nos 1 & 4 Coy moved to dumps at GODE. 9 took over construction of mining frames. No 2 Coy moved to MT des CATS and took over construction of deviation road (KNOX'S CAUSEWAY) to LA MANCHE. H.Q. & No 3 Coy returned to Horse Lines at EECKE.	
	31st		The whole Coy was due to go out to rest. Move cancelled owing to retirement of GERMANS from the line opposite our front. Nos 2 & 4 Coy return to EECKE. No 1 Coy remained at GODE Dumps	[signature] Capt RE

Army Form C. 2118.

WAR DIARY
or
INTELLIGENCE SUMMARY.
(Erase heading not required.)

Confidential

War Diary
of the
122nd Field Coy. Royal Engineers
36th Div
1st September to 30th September
1918

E. Whittle
Capt RE
O.C. 122 Field Coy RE

Army Form C. 2118.

WAR DIARY
or
INTELLIGENCE SUMMARY.
(Erase heading not required.)

Instructions regarding War Diaries and Intelligence Summaries are contained in F. S. Regs., Part II. and the Staff Manual respectively. Title pages will be prepared in manuscript.

Place	Date	Hour	Summary of Events and Information	Remarks and references to Appendices
Field	1/9/18		27/025927 H.Q. and 3 Sections moved to farm at Ecole employed cleaning equipment instruction on Lewis Gun. repairs to Wagons &c	
"	2/9/18		H.Q and 3 Sections moved to M71 a 61	
"	3rd & 5th		Repairing billets. Lewis Gun instruction, bayonet fighting & drill Major Smyth proceeded on leave to U.K on 3rd Capt M.H.Lee assumed command.	
	(6th)/8		Repairing billets. Lewis Gun instruction, bayonet fighting. A.T.S inoculation	
	8th		Lieut E.A. Wheatley arrived from 3rd Fd Coy RE to serve over duties as Section Commander. Commenced making accommodation for Sect H.Q at F.fans Eppel	
	9th		"	
	10th		Capt M.H.Lee M.C. R.E left to command 202nd Fd Cy RE Capt E.A Whalley assumed duties as Second-in-Command	
	11th		No 4 Section returned No 1 Section on R.E Dump Godendorsvelde work and Sk edward	
	12th to 15th		Making accommodation for Sect H.Q at F.fans Eppel. repair of billets &c	
	16th		No 4 Section returned from R.E Dump Godendorsvelde	
	17th			
	19th		20 on 12th to 15th Capt J.H. Allen RE joined from work on defences in Second Army to be attached for 2 months	
	20th		Coy relieved by 202nd Field Cy RE & moved to S27/Q25 a 7.9.	

Army Form C. 2118.

WAR DIARY
or
INTELLIGENCE SUMMARY.
(Erase heading not required.)

Instructions regarding War Diaries and Intelligence Summaries are contained in F. S. Regs., Part II. and the Staff Manual respectively. Title pages will be prepared in manuscript.

Place	Date	Hour	Summary of Events and Information	Remarks and references to Appendices
Field	21st		Inspection of Arms & Box respirators Drill etc.	
	22nd		Major A Smyth reported from leave relieved Lieut A.G.C.G. Woodhedley as O.C.	
			Coy moved to S29/A 2 1 & 2. 9	
	23rd		Commenced work under C.E. 2nd Corps. Building Stables & Accommodation to 29 Inf Train.	
			1 O.R. wounded by bomb from enemy aircraft	
	24th to 25th		Building stables etc. for 29th Inf Train	
	26th		Lieut R Charlesworth RE transferred to 150th Field Cy RE. took us on 23rd-25th	
	27th		Work as on 23rd to 26th	
	28th		Coy moved to 29 H.Q. @ 10.00 - dismounted branch by rail. Mounted branch by road	
			2nd Man RE & 3rd Lt Evans RE. Temporarily transferred to 1/4 @ Fd Cy RE.	
	29th		4 Sections moved to S'28/JS Central Coy employed repairing roads	
	30th		Coy employed repairing roads	

CONFIDENTIAL

WAR DIARY.
of
122nd Field Coy Royal Engineers.
36th Divn
1st Oct - 31st Oct
1918

WAR DIARY or INTELLIGENCE SUMMARY

Army Form C. 2118.

Place	Date	Hour	Summary of Events and Information	Remarks and references to Appendices
Field	1/10/18		To camp H 6 & 7.5	
			4 Section move to J 8 central, employed on roads	
	2nd		ditto	
	3rd		ditto	
	4th		4 Section & H.Q. moved to J 18 & 5 B	
	5th		Nos 2 & 4 Section employed on roads	
	6th		4 Section on roads	
	7th		ditto	
	8th		ditto	
	9th		4 Section on roads. Also German 5.9 Howitzer extracted from shellhole at J 23 d 8.4	
	10th		4 Section on roads & fifty railway sleepers	
			Also 11 St Toulon & 10 OR went forward and mined	
	11th		4 Section on roads	
	12th		ditto	
			ditto	
			out assembly trench	
			Major Smyth RE rejoined from o/c CRE	
	13th		Issue of clothing. Deficiencies in tool kits made up	
	15th		Coy moved to L 13. d 8 2 (BECELAERE)	
	16th		O.C. Capt Wheatley lifts Tagan Toulon & 2 Wt RE & 16 OR per Sect left at 4 AM to build	
			L Ts of COURTRAI casualties :- 11 St Toulon RE killed, Capt Wheatley & 11 St Tagan wounded	
			2 OR killed, 1 wounded & missing & 14 wounded by M.G. fire. Repair attacked	
	17th		Company moved at 9 AM from L 13 & 8 2 to G 2 c 2 0	
	18th		Kit, rifle & respirator inspection	
	19th		D.T.O	
	20th		Coy moved to LENDELEDE (A 17 & 11)	
	21st		Training Kit inspections	
	22nd		Coy gathered in Belgian clothing as was	

Army Form C. 2118.

WAR DIARY
or
INTELLIGENCE SUMMARY.

(Erase heading not required.)

Instructions regarding War Diaries and Intelligence Summaries are contained in F. S. Regs., Part II. and the Staff Manual respectively. Title pages will be prepared in manuscript.

Place	Date	Hour	Summary of Events and Information	Remarks and references to Appendices
	23/9/18		Reconnaissance in event of taking over bridge transference from 121 & 150 Field Coys	
	24"		Training	
	25"		Coy moved to C.13.C.5.3	
	26"		Training	
	27"		Capt Mitchell RE seconded from base, took over 2ic in command (11/8.0 wTrain 511st Searchgts arrived from base.	
	28"		Coy moved to 29/B.13.C.6.3. (LENDELEDE)	
	29"		Coy moved to 28/B.24.a.3.6. (LAUWE)	
	30"		Overhaul of tools & pontoon equipment. Training	
	31.		Training & Sports. Mem Ch	

On the morning of the 16th October 1918, it was arranged to bridge the River Lys at Courtrai (Sheet 29/H.25.d.1.7.).

The 122nd Field Coy. R.E., was detailed to throw the bridge across the River, while the Commanding Officer of the 9th R. Irish Fusiliers made all arrangements for landing and covering parties, also for a smoke screen and Trench mortar fire on selected targets.

The artillery were also to co-operate by putting down a barrage on a high bank, about 200 yards on the right front, but failed to do so. The smoke screen on the right was poor, but might have been sufficient, if the artillery barrage had been provided as promised.

At 12-30 hours the pontoons were brought forward to within 30 yards of the River bank behind houses. The pontoons were unloaded, and all stores laid out in readiness under the shelter of a wood pile, by 13-00 hours.

At 14.00 hours the smoke screen was put down, and the T.M. Batteries and Lewis Guns opened fire on selected targets.

At 14.05 hours it was considered that the smoke screen was thick enough, and bridging could commence.

2 Lieut. J.J.A. Fagan R.E. took the first party down to the River with a half pontoon, and launched it successfully. A Lewis Gun team and three Riflemen were ferried across in this, and a Sapper party landed, who put in a rope anchorage. 2 Lieut Fagan superintended the further ferrying of Infantry until he was wounded.

Meanwhile, 2 Lieut A.J. Towlson, R.E. had launched the next boat and started bridging.

All available infantry having been ferried across, the boat

Army Form C. 2118.

Vol 3 f

WAR DIARY
or
INTELLIGENCE SUMMARY.
(Erase heading not required.)

Instructions regarding War Diaries and Intelligence Summaries are contained in F. S. Regs., Part II. and the Staff Manual respectively. Title pages will be prepared in manuscript.

War Diary
of the
261 Field Company R.E.
36th Division

1st November — 30th November 1918.

Confidential

Place	Date	Hour	Summary of Events and Information	Remarks and references to Appendices

WAR DIARY
or
INTELLIGENCE SUMMARY.
(Erase heading not required.)

Army Form C. 2118.

Instructions regarding War Diaries and Intelligence Summaries are contained in F.S. Regs., Part II. and the Staff Manual respectively. Title pages will be prepared in manuscript.

Place	Date	Hour	Summary of Events and Information	Remarks and references to Appendices
Lacune S26/R14a5,7	1/11/18		Coy employed in vocational training, rifle drill, physical exercise (football) Major Smyth went to Corps Pick Minia — Light Bridging (equipment)	
	2/11/18		Rifle drill & physical training in morning — eight Bridging — afternoon	
	3/11/18		Coy moved with Bn. troops to Maroeuni and took billets at S/19 S.2 3 9 5.6	
Maroeuni S.2 3 a 5.6 Sheet 44	4/11/18		Sappers move to move comfortable billets. Coy bathed.	
	5/11/18		Training — Rifle drill, physical training & potoway	
	6/11/18			
	7/11/18			
	8/11/18		Route March in morning. Football afternoon Honours & Awards for bridge at Croisilles 16/10/18 Major S. Smyth — Bar to M.C. Capt S. Whalley M.C. "Lt A. Tongers M.C. Sgt Bloom D.C.M Sgt " Wright " Spr " Sherall " " E. Sake "	
	9/11/18		Drill in morning. Lecture by M.O. surveyed in afternoon Coy moved to Autoyne for heavy bridging under C.E. I Corps	
Autoyne Sq/W8d 9,8	10/11/18		Work on heavy potoon bridge & across Schiedt Row at Sq V.10 c 5.7 Coy worked w/self rfts two with a Sd Coy of 207th Div =	
	11/11/18		"Lt R. Haughu to Hospital with influenza	

Army Form C. 2118.

WAR DIARY
or
INTELLIGENCE SUMMARY.
(Erase heading not required.)

Instructions regarding War Diaries and Intelligence Summaries are contained in F. S. Regs., Part II. and the Staff Manual respectively. Title pages will be prepared in manuscript.

Place	Date	Hour	Summary of Events and Information	Remarks and references to Appendices
Antwyn Sqy/V8 & q/18	13, 14, 15, 16	8/11/18	Coy. employed in erection of heavy girder bridge at Sqy/V2 & b z.z. Working in conjunction with 150 Td Coy R.E. who took morning shift from 6.o.am. to 12 noon. We took afternoon shift from 12.oo hrs to 18.oo hrs.	
	17/11/18	8	Battle and inspection by medical officer in morning. Interior Economy football in afternoon.	
Anavran Sqy/S23 a 5.6	18/11/18	8	Coy. moved to Anavran. SS. 3 a 5.6.	
	19/11/18, 20/11/18	8	Drills & inspections. Lecture by "C" Section on Demolitions.	
	21/11/18, 22, 23, 24, 25, 26	8	Battle at 2.2.T. Instruction given in doctrinal scheme.	
	27/11/18	8	Drills & inspections, Interior sitions and Inter Coy. football.	
	28/11/18	8	Route March.	
	29/11/18, 30	8/11/18	Coy. employed in demolition of old German bakery in a factory close by. Inspection by M.O. Drills & inspections.	

J. Mitchell
Capt R.E.

1/12/18

Army Form C. 2118.

WAR DIARY
or
INTELLIGENCE SUMMARY.
(Erase heading not required.)

CONFIDENTIAL

WAR DIARY
of the
122ND Field Company R.E.
36th Division.
1st December — 31st December 1918.

Place	Date	Hour	Summary of Events and Information	Remarks and references to Appendices

Army Form C. 2118.

WAR DIARY
or
INTELLIGENCE SUMMARY.
(Erase heading not required.)

Instructions regarding War Diaries and Intelligence Summaries are contained in F. S. Regs., Part II. and the Staff Manual respectively. Title pages will be prepared in manuscript.

Place	Date	Hour	Summary of Events and Information	Remarks and references to Appendices
Maresco Sq1/S23a5.6	1/1/18		Church parade in morning. Soccer game against M. Guns. Bn in afternoon. Result drawn	
	2/1/18		Drill & cleaning of equipment	
	3/1/18		Bn Commanders inspection of "D" Coy in morning	
	4/1/18		Bn Commanders inspection of "A" Coy. Tug-of-war ground prepared. Drills & presentation of Tramway instead	
	5/1/18		Running, Platoon & Shining. Afternoon drew against 16th S.R. Result 3-1 in our favor	
			Route march. Following men have been selected on football committee. C.Q.M.S. Young	
				Cpl Garritt
				Spr Ferguson
				Cpr McIntyre
				Cpr McCleary
	6/1/18		Bn Commanders inspection at Hallencourt area ground	
	7/1/18		All men on work & fatigues. P.M. D's inspection of ammunition & attention to equipment in order	
	8/1/18		Church parade. Bombs from D. Coy. under Capt Hughes & Lt Shelfer proceeded to	
			Hallincourt to work in magazine. C.R.S. 39th Div —	
	9/1/18		Work and Fatigues. Following distinctions found during de Guerre (Bronze Star) —	
				awarded to T/Lt. T.R. Benson no. 57530. Sgt. Sturgeon
				Capt. to 8t Brie for X mas purchases
	10/1/18		Work & Fatigues. Battn in afternoon	
	11/1/18		Drill & cleaning of equipment for Corps Commanders inspection	

Army Form C. 2118.

WAR DIARY
or
INTELLIGENCE SUMMARY.
(Erase heading not required.)

Instructions regarding War Diaries and Intelligence Summaries are contained in F. S. Regs., Part II. and the Staff Manual respectively. Title pages will be prepared in manuscript.

Place	Date	Hour	Summary of Events and Information	Remarks and references to Appendices
Havenow S24/S23 a56	12/12/18		Corps Commanders Inspection cancelled owing to weather, took to fatigues around hutt	
	13/12/18		Shooting at Ranges in morning, Musketry Training afternoon	
	14/12/18		Work & fatigues	
	15/12/18		Pints & cleaning equipment for Corps Commanders inspection	
	16/12/18		Corps Commanders Inspection 1st Hallnon Flying Ground	
	17/12/18		Fatigues in morning. Soccer against 109 Fd Amb. & afternoon. Result 3-1 in our favour	
	18/12/18		Work & fatigues in & battalion v 111 $\frac{5}{6}$ in Bn. Jalnage as any staining Cup	
	19/12/18		Works fatigues	
	20/12/18		Work & fatigues	
	21/12/18		Work & fatigues. Soccer match against 1st R.I.R. Result 3-1 in our favour	
	22/12/18		Church service. Detachment returned from bridging at Halluin	
	23/12/18		Work & fatigues	
	24/12/18			
	25/12/18		Christmas Day - Popery Day, No work. Xmas dinner for men at noon as Xmas day. Concert at night. Football on Xmas morning against 121 Fd Coy. Result 3-0 in our favour	
	26/12/18			
	27/12/18		Work & fatigues	
	28/12/18		Work & fatigues	
	29/12/18		Church services	
	30/12/18 31/12/18		Work & fatigues. Coy photograph taken on 31/12/18	

A Mitchell Capt RE

36

Army Form C. 2118.

WAR DIARY
or
INTELLIGENCE SUMMARY.
(Erase heading not required.)

VB 40

WAR DIARY.

OF THE

122ND FIELD COMPANY. R.E.

36TH DIVISION

1ST JANUARY — 31ST JANUARY 1919.

Whitelaw Capt R.E.
for O.C. 122nd Field Coy.R.E.

CONFIDENTIAL

Place	Date	Hour	Summary of Events and Information	Remarks and references to Appendices

Instructions regarding War Diaries and Intelligence Summaries are contained in F. S. Regs., Part II. and the Staff Manual respectively. Title pages will be prepared in manuscript.

WAR DIARY
or
INTELLIGENCE SUMMARY.
(Erase heading not required.)

Army Form C. 2118.

Place	Date	Hour	Summary of Events and Information	Remarks and references to Appendices
Mouscron.	1/1/19		New Years Day observed as a holiday except for [illegible] fatigues	
	2/1/19		Drill & musketry in the morning, recreational training afternoon	
	3/1/19		Work & fatigues. Medical inspection	
	4/1/19		Work & fatigues	
	5/1/19		Church parades in morning	
	6-11/1/19		Work & fatigues, Medical inspection on 11/1/19. 2nd Lt Munson joined Coy 7/1/19. 2 men for demobilization on 11th	
	12/1/19		Lt Munson & 25 O.R. to Roubaix by bus for Army Commander's Church Parade. Following awards of the Belgian Croix de Guerre – Major W. Smyth M.C. R.E. 57686 C.Q.M.S. V. Morgan. 3 men for demobilization	
	13/1/19		Work & fatigues, Whist Drive at night. 2 men for Demobilization	
	13-18/1/19		Work & fatigues. Medical inspection on 17th	
	19/1/19		Church parade in morning. C.S.M. Russell left to be a/R.S.M. 3rd Divn	
	20/1/19		Work & fatigues. 8 men for demobilization	
	21/1/19		Work & fatigues, Nos 1 & 2 sections amalgamated under Lt Benson. 4 men for demobilization	
	22/1/19		Work & fatigues in morning. Divl Semi-final Soccer in afternoon. 1?? Fd Coy vs. 15 R.I.R. Score 1 – 5. 4 Lt Schofield & 60 O.R. for demobilization	

D. D. & L., London, E.C.
(A8004) Wt. W1771/M2031 750,000 5/17 Sch. 52 Forms/C2.118/14

Army Form C. 2118.

WAR DIARY
or
INTELLIGENCE SUMMARY.
(Erase heading not required.)

Place	Date	Hour	Summary of Events and Information	Remarks and references to Appendices
Morvaux	23/1/19		Work & fatigues. Meritorious service Medal awarded to No 57687 P/Sgt. L. Ferguson	
	24/1/19		3 men for demolition. "N" Officers & hospital ack.	
	25/1/19		Work & fatigues. Medical Inspection	
	26/1/19		Work & fatigues	
			Church parade & O.R. for investigation	
	27/1/19 to 31/1/19		Work & fatigues. "N" O.R. for investigation. 3 & 4 Sections amalgamated for working.	

Westerlee Capt PE

C/482
31.1.19

Instructions regarding War Diaries and Intelligence Summaries are contained in F. S. Regs, Part II. and the Staff Manual respectively. Title pages will be prepared in manuscript.

Army Form C. 2118.

WAR DIARY
or
INTELLIGENCE SUMMARY.
(Erase heading not required.)

Vol 41

CONFIDENTIAL

WAR DIARY

OF THE

122ND FIELD COMPANY R.E.

From FEBRUARY 1st 19

To FEBRUARY 28th 19

M[signature]
Capt R.E.
For O.C. 122 Field Coy R.E.

Army Form C. 2118.

WAR DIARY
or
INTELLIGENCE SUMMARY.
(Erase heading not required.)

Instructions regarding War Diaries and Intelligence Summaries are contained in F. S. Regs., Part II. and the Staff Manual respectively. Title pages will be prepared in manuscript.

Place	Date	Hour	Summary of Events and Information	Remarks and references to Appendices
Maroeuil	1/7/19		Work & Fatigues	
	2/4/3		Work & Fatigues	
	3/7/9		Inspection of rifles & Lewis Guns by Army Inspector. Work & Fatigues	
	4/7/19		11+ O.R. trgsn from hospital	
	5/7/19			
	6/7/19		Work & Fatigues	
	7/7/19			
	8/7/19			
	9/7/19		Church Service	
	10/7/19		Work & Fatigues. Battn.	
	11/7/19		Work & Fatigues. 1 Lt Evers & 40 O.Rs. for demobilization	
	12/7/19		Work & Fatigues	
	13/7/19		Work & Fatigues. 5 O.Rs for demobilization	
	14/7/19		Work & Fatigues	
	15/7/19		Church Parade	
	16/7/19		Work & Fatigues. 30 O.Rs for demobilization. 1 Brn to England. Draft constituting demobilized men	
	17/7/19		Work & Fatigues	
	18/7/19			
	19/7/19			

Army Form C. 2118.

WAR DIARY
or
INTELLIGENCE SUMMARY.

(Erase heading not required.)

Instructions regarding War Diaries and Intelligence Summaries are contained in F. S. Regs., Part II. and the Staff Manual respectively. Title pages will be prepared in manuscript.

Place	Date	Hour	Summary of Events and Information	Remarks and references to Appendices
Tournai	2/1/19		Work & fatigues	
	5/1/19		Church parade	
	23/1/19			
	24/1/19		Work & fatigues. Baths 2 & 4 th	
	25/1/19			
	27/1/19			
	28/1/19		Work & fatigues	
	29/1/19			

www.ingramcontent.com/pod-product-compliance
Lightning Source LLC
Chambersburg PA
CBHW081534160426
43191CB00011B/1759